# IELTS Writing 9.0 Proficiency ©

## Task 2:

## Master IELTS Essays

**+ FREE IELTS WRITING VIDEO COURSE + BAND 9 ESSAY TEMPLATES. Essay Writing & Grammar for IELTS Academic + General Writing Task 2.**

IELTS Book

IELTS Writing Books Series ©

By

*Marc Roche*

&

*IELTS Writing Consultants*

Copyright © 2021 **Marc Roche and IELTS Writing Consultants**

## PREMIUM ©UDEMY IELTS WRITING COURSE DISCOUNT

https://bit.ly/3OF0v0h

No part of this IELTS book may be reproduced, distributed, or transmitted in any form or by any means, including photocopying, recording, or other electronic or mechanical methods, or by any information storage and retrieval system without the prior written permission of the publisher, except in the case of very brief quotations embodied in critical reviews and certain other noncommercial uses permitted by copyright law.

**IELTS is a registered trademark of the University of Cambridge ESOL, the British Council, and IDP Education Australia.**

*Master IELTS Writing Band 9.0 Essays*

## ABOUT THE AUTHOR 3

## ABOUT THIS BOOK 5

## IELTS WRITING TASK 1 PROFICIENCY BY MARC ROCHE 11

## FREE IELTS WRITING COURSE 14

## INTRODUCTION 16

IELTS ACADEMIC WRITING OVERVIEW 17
IELTS GENERAL WRITING OVERVIEW 18
ABOUT IELTS WRITING TASK 2 19
HOW MANY WORDS SHOULD I WRITE IN MY IELTS ESSAY? 20
SENTENCE STRUCTURES 22
PARAGRAPH STRUCTURES 23
UNDERSTANDING THE TOPIC AND THE TASK 24
THE BEGINNING OF THE ESSAY 25
EXPRESSING THE IMPORTANCE OF THE TOPIC 29
EFFICIENCY 31
SHOWING BALANCE IN YOUR ESSAY 36
FOCUS ON THE TOPIC AND THE TASK 39
COMMON MISTAKES IN THE IELTS ESSAY 41
HOW TO EVALUATE YOUR IELTS WRITING 50
BRAINSTORMING AND PLANNING RECAP 52
THE FIVE MAIN TYPES OF IELTS ESSAY 53

## OPINION ESSAYS 54

TWO TYPES OF OPINION ESSAY QUESTION: 55
HOW TO AGREE 100% WITH ONE SIDE 57
HOW TO GIVE A BALANCED OPINION ESSAY (TAKING IDEAS FROM BOTH SIDES) 83

## ADVANTAGES & DISADVANTAGES ESSAY 95

Marc Roche

## PROBLEM & SOLUTION ESSAY 120

## DISCUSSION ESSAY 146

## TWO-PART ESSAY QUESTION 168

USEFUL PHRASES 197
EXPRESSING VIEWS 198
REFUTING AN ARGUMENT 199
PROVIDING SUPPORT 199
DEFINING AND EXPLAINING 200
USE THESE CAREFULLY 200
USE MODERATELY 201
OTHER USEFUL PHRASES 202
INTRODUCING A FALSE ARGUMENT 204
DESTROYING A FALSE ARGUMENT 204
SUGGESTING A CORRECT ARGUMENT 204

## PRIVATE IELTS WRITING ADVANCED BAND 9 COURSE ON ©UDEMY 206

## FREE IELTS WRITING COURSE: ADVANCED WRITING (FOUNDATION LEVEL FOR IELTS) 207

# About the Author

**Marc Roche**

Marc is originally from the UK and currently lives in Spain. He is a father, teacher, trainer, writer, and entrepreneur. He has collaborated with organizations such as the British Council, IDP, the Royal Melbourne Institute of Technology (RMIT), and the University of Technology Sydney, among others. Marc has also worked as a corporate trainer with multinationals such as Nike and GlaxoSmithKline. When he is not taking care of his son, writing books, or working on his businesses, Marc likes to practice martial arts, socialize, spend time with friends and family, and watch football.

# Learn more about Marc at

http://www.amazon.com/author/marcroche

## YOUTUBE

https://www.youtube.com/channel/UCCekbxL4WYFO2dOGxL4fQTQ

# About This Book

"This book is your map to success in the IELTS Writing test."

# TYPES OF IELTS ESSAY COVERED IN THIS BOOK:

1. Opinion Essay (Agree or Disagree)

2. Advantages & Disadvantages Essay

3. Problem & Solution Essay

4. Discussion Essay

5. Two-part Essay Question

# ABOUT THE BOOK + FREE COURSE

**IELTS Writing 9.0 Proficiency Task 2: Master IELTS Essays © + FREE IELTS WRITING VIDEO COURSE**

**IELTS Writing is Too Important to Mess Up**

★★★★★ **"This book is your map to success in the IELTS Writing test."**

**TYPES OF IELTS ESSAY COVERED IN THIS BOOK:**

- Opinion Essay (Agree or Disagree)
- Advantages & Disadvantages Essay
- Problem & Solution Essay
- Discussion Essay
- Two-part Essay Question

*"IELTS Writing 9.0 Proficiency Task 2: Master IELTS Essays © + FREE IELTS WRITING VIDEO COURSE + BAND 9 ESSAY TEMPLATES. Essay Writing & Grammar for IELTS Academic + General Writing Task 2. IELTS Book 1".*

IELTS Writing Academic + General Task 2 is vital in order to get the highest band scores in the official IELTS test, as well as to increase your general level of English. Master essay writing & grammar for the IELTS Academic & General Training tests in a short space of time with this special edition IELTS writing book by Marc Roche, crammed full of highly focused and easy-to-follow instructions, activities and secret tactics. *"IELTS Writing 9.0 Proficiency"* will gently guide you through advanced level IELTS writing, with specialized IELTS practice activities and tips and tricks for the test. *"IELTS Writing 9.0 Proficiency"* is perfect for ambitious IELTS candidates who don't want to waste time researching and learning all the unnecessary jargon that's usually included in traditional IELTS writing books. This book will make your preparation more effective and less time-consuming.

## ABOUT THE BOOK + FREE COURSE

*"IELTS Writing 9.0 Proficiency Task 2: Master IELTS Essays* © *+ FREE IELTS WRITING VIDEO COURSE"*, is a fully comprehensive self-study IELTS Academic Writing and IELTS General Writing essay course for candidates who need to get the highest band scores in the IELTS exam (Bands 7.0-9.0). This IELTS Writing book includes Band 9 Essay Templates, practice exercises, language, and strategy tips for ALL types of IELTS Essay, as well as a FREE Online IELTS Writing Course for highly motivated candidates who wish to maximize their preparation.

*IELTS Writing 9.0 Proficiency Task 2: Master IELTS Essays* © *+ FREE IELTS WRITING VIDEO COURSE* is suitable for both the IELTS Academic and the IELTS General written exams, and it simplifies the process of learning high-level essay writing. The **SUCCESS MAP** revealed within this book guides you step-by-step with simple explanations, high-level language, expert tips, templates, and specialist exercises. By following the instructions in this IELTS preparation book, upper-intermediate and advanced English students can comfortably reach an IELTS Band 9.0 score in the essay.

## IELTS Academic Writing & IELTS Writing General Training

Students are guided step-by-step through the process of writing for the IELTS Academic test with exercises, secret tactics, explanations, and examples for:

- Opinion Essay (Agree or Disagree)
- Advantages & Disadvantages Essay
- Problem & Solution Essay
- Discussion Essay
- Two-part Essay Question

## WHAT YOU WILL GET FROM THIS BOOK:

- Learn **how to structure and organize all types of IELTS Academic and General essays**.
- **Quickly develop fluency and confidence** in producing proficient IELTS Band 9 essays under exam conditions!

- Get **specialized IELTS writing skills** with exercises and **exam secrets**.
- Learn **how to apply a wide range of tools** in your responses.
- **The chapters, expert tricks, and exercises inside this book, if followed correctly, will help you reach a Band 9.0 in the IELTS essay.**

# IELTS WRITING TASK 1 Proficiency by Marc Roche

**MASTER IELTS WRITING: TASK 1 (ACADEMIC & GENERAL SUPER PACK)**

# IELTS BAND 9 WRITING COURSE

## https://bit.ly/3OF0v0h

## Available from Amazon

IELTS Vocabulary Masterclass 8.5 (BOOK 1)

IELTS Grammar Masterclass 8.5

IELTS Vocabulary Masterclass 8.5 (BOOK 2)

IELTS Vocabulary Masterclass 8.5 (BOOK 3)

IELTS Speaking Masterplan 8.5

Master IELTS Writing Band 9 Essays

# FREE IELTS Writing Course

Claim your FREE Course Worth $67 at the end of this book!

# Introduction

*"One language sets you in a corridor for life. Two languages open every door along the way."* - Frank Smith

# IELTS Academic Writing Overview

Length: 60 minutes

### Academic Writing Test

| Task | Word count | Advised Timing | Task description |
|---|---|---|---|
| 1 | 150 | 20 mins | Describe visual information such as bar tables, charts, graphs, maps, or diagrams. |
| 2 | 250 | 40 mins | Present arguments and opinions in a discursive essay about an issue. |

**TIP:** TIP: Although the exam instructions tell you to write "at least" 250 in the essay, don't write a lot more.

# IELTS General Writing Overview

Length: 60 minutes

## General Writing Test

| Task | Word count | Advised Timing | Task description |
|---|---|---|---|
| 1 | 150 | 20 mins | The candidate is presented with a situation and is asked to write a letter requesting information, or explaining an issue. The letter may be personal, semi-formal or formal in style. |
| 2 | 250 | 40 mins | Presenting arguments and opinions in a discursive essay about a topical issue. |

Source: IELTS.org

**TIP:** The exam says to write a 'minimum of 150/250 words but don't write much more. Aim for 10 or 20 words more at the most.

# About IELTS Writing Task 2

- The Writing component of IELTS Academic and IELTS General has two tasks. This book will only focus on Task 2, which is the essay.
- Task 2 is exactly the same in both the Academic exam and the General exam.
- You will need to write an essay in response to an opinion, an argument, or a problem.
- Your essay must be written in formal English.

# How Many Words Should I Write in My IELTS Essay?

- In task 2, you should write at least 250 words

- You should spend 40 minutes on it

## Two Common Problems in the Exam…

### Problem 1- NOT ENOUGH Words:

- Less than 250 words MIGHT lower your score (you might not explain your ideas very well).

### Problem 2- TOO MANY Words:

- You might be using too many words.

- You might be trying to express too much information.

### This means:

- You might run out of time during the exam.

- The longer your essay is, the more probability you have of making grammar and vocabulary mistakes.

- If you write too many words in Task 2, you will have less time to complete task 1.

## Sentence Structures

*"The English language is an arsenal of weapons. If you are going to brandish them without checking to see whether or not they are loaded, you must expect to have them explode in your face from time to time."* ~ Stephen Fry

- Every sentence has its own purpose.

- Treat each sentence like **GOLD**: there should be no useless sentences in your essay

- Plan your sentences: you need to make sure every piece of your essay fits together

- Be concise: don't fall into the trap of trying to make every sentence longer and more complicated just to fill space.

- Write your essay like a human being is going to read it!

# Paragraph Structures

### A paragraph normally has three parts:

1. One sentence to introduce the general topic we will write about in the paragraph (you also normally need to link the first sentence to the previous paragraph).

2. Two or three sentences that develop the topic in more detail. In the IELTS exam, you usually need to include evidence, examples, and details about the topic or argument.

3. A concluding sentence that either finishes the topic (or links it to the next paragraph).

# Understanding the Topic and the Task

- Make sure you understand what the topic or subject of questions is. Underline the keywords if necessary.

- Read the questions carefully to identify exactly what you need to.

- Focus on the question itself, not on what you want to write about.

**There usually are three ways the essay can be presented in the exam. Let's take the example of space exploration:**

Type 1: Two **opposite views** to discuss:

"Some people believe that more funds should be invested in space exploration, as it is a vital form of investigation for the future of humanity. In contrast, others believe it is a waste of vital funding that could otherwise be used towards more essential projects here on earth. "

Type 2: "Two **opposite views** to discuss using the word *should* in the instruction.

"Should more money be invested into space exploration, or should it be used towards more important projects here on earth?"

Type 3: A **statement** to discuss:

- "Paying for space exploration is a waste of vital funding which could otherwise be used towards more important projects here on earth."

# The Beginning of the Essay

To get the highest grades in the IELTS exam, the essay has to introduce the topic, so you must begin with a relatively general statement. However, the trick is not to over-generalise; otherwise, the statement becomes meaningless and can be annoying to read. For example, the following first sentence from an essay is meaningless, and the structure used is not appropriate.

*There are those who argue that water is necessary for human life, and therefore water shortage is one of the most important problems in the world.*

## Comments

Water is vital to human life, and this is an absolute fact, not something that people can argue about. The student wanted to use *'There are those who argue that,'* but this structure is wrong for the meaning of the sentence. The statement is also too general, and it is not clear what this essay is about.

## Possible improvement

*Water shortages affect millions of people worldwide each year, and there is evidence that suggests that they are becoming increasingly difficult to tackle due to climate change.*

In the comments section above, you will see that it is a bad idea to memorize words or structures ('There are those who argue that,' 'nobody would dispute the fact that…' etc.) to insert your ideas into. As discussed in previous chapters, each sentence and paragraph are like a house that needs logical, solid foundations before you decorate it. It is better to start with your ideas and then think about how you can express them best.

## Connecting Paragraphs to Each Other

When you start a new paragraph, you tell the reader that the previous point is finished, and you are creating something new. Nevertheless, this new paragraph is not disconnected from the previous one, and you need to communicate to the reader what the connection is. For instance, if you start with *However, there are those who argue that violence is not something we learn from television and computer games...* then the structure you have used signals to the reader that you are discussing a different argument (*'However,'*) which contradicts the previous ideas, and *'there are those who argue that..',* which is expressed by other people, not you. You have communicated a lot of information to the reader with only seven words (*However, there are those who argue that...*). This is one of the definitions of good writing. Effective, while using as few words as possible to maintain clarity.

### *"Another argument is that...."*

If you start a new paragraph with the phrase '*Another argument in favour of stricter laws is that crime is directly related to...*' then you are signalling to the reader that you are changing to a different argument ('*Another*') with the same purpose ('*in favour of..*').

### To give more specific information, use '*This argument ...*'.

This is a handy structure to learn, and it can be adapted to many different contexts.

The words in the box below are all useful examples of words like 'argument,' which you can use with the word 'this' (or 'these' in plural) to specify more information.

| analysis | approach | concept | context |
|---|---|---|---|
| data | definition | environment | evidence |
| factor | issue | problem | function |
| measure | method | period | policy |
| principle | procedure | process | theory |
| response | sector | structure | interpretation |

**Here is an example of how we can use this structure in an essay.**

*There is no doubt that corruption is the most crucial point to focus on because it originates from positions of power. Corruption can take many shapes and forms, such as political, which involves crimes in a country's legal system and within the police, and economic, for example, by misusing tax money. All the evidence suggests that countries with corrupt governments are not able to develop as fast as countries where there is less corruption.*

*These factors [...].*

**OR**

*This negative environment [...].*

The first sentence of a paragraph is vital, as it shows how it connects with the overall structure and can signal what will happen next.

When you practice writing, always check that your essay is logical by underlining the most important sentences in each paragraph. You should be able to understand the whole essay only by reading those sentences. If you can't, you need to make changes.

# Expressing the Importance of the Topic

**Superlatives** can be useful to indicate that the topic is important:

| | | causes of ... | is ... |
|---|---|---|---|
| (one of) **the most** | | problems of ... | |
| | significant | conditions for ... | are ... |
| (some of) **the most** | important | aspects of ... | |

| | | | causes of ... |
|---|---|---|---|
| | | | problems of ... |
| | | significant | conditions for ... |
| ... is | (one of) **the most** | important | aspects of ... |

The following **adjective** and noun combinations can also be useful:

## Adjective - Noun combinations

| increasing concern | an **important** part | a **key** role/ factor | a **great/major** problem |
|---|---|---|---|
| a **central** area of | a **commo** problem | an **increasing** need/concern | **heightened** awareness |
| **rapid** development | a **dramatic** increase | **renewed/ unpreceden-ted** interest | a **serious** effect/ impact on |

You can also use the following combinations with **adverbs**:

| is becoming **increasingly** important | is becoming **increasingly** challenging | has been **extensively** resear ched |
|---|---|---|

# Efficiency

Efficient writing expresses an idea, opinion, reason, or consequence without using too many words. Many students make a big mistake because they try to fill the page with words thinking this will make them finish the essay sooner and look good. After all, it means they know a lot. This is entirely wrong for most, if not all, exams, whether it's the IELTS or a university exam. Always use the minimum number of words possible, and do not repeat yourself.

According to Google, the definition of efficiency is: *"maximum productivity with minimum wasted effort or expense."* In your writing, this means few words but lots of meaning.

**Note:** remember that in the IELTS, the word count indicated in the exam is a minimum, not a maximum, so you still need to reach this minimum, or you will be penalised, but you should avoid repetition and meaningless sentences by carefully proofreading your writing before you finish.

## Using nouns in your essay

If you pay attention to the best essay examples and the best academic writing in general, you will notice that many noun phrases are used.

Here is an example:

*"At an investigative level, the availability of digital resources, simulators, and other tools provide the researcher with increased access to information. "*

A large portion of that sentence is made up of nouns. Using nouns is hugely efficient, whereas using verbs can be long and repetitive in an essay or description sometimes. (Ideally, you should combine both structures to add variety and power to your writing.)

For example, you use less space if you are talking about processes without describing the action:

| Temperature increase | They have increased the temperature |
|---|---|
| Efficiency increase (increase in efficiency) | They have increased the efficiency |

# Exercise 2

Change the sentences by using nouns instead of verbs where possible.

The trick is to find the verbs first, then transform some of them into nouns, e.g.:

*The area __would benefit__ if businesses __increased__ the amount they __produced__.*

*The area would benefit from __an increase__ in __business productivity/business production__.*

1. The local government should train their employees better so that they can be more efficient.

   ................................................................

   ................................................................

2. There is a difference between cultures, so they need to communicate by using different strategies.

   ................................................................

   ................................................................

3. If governments around the world implement this strategy, they may reduce pollution.

........................................................

........................................................

4. If they recycle waste, they may have a better chance of reducing poverty in the area.

........................................................

........................................................

# Master IELTS Writing Band 9 Essays

# Suggested Answers

### Exercise 2

1. *Better employee training would increase the local government's efficiency. / With better employee training, the local government's efficiency would increase.*

2. *Cultural differences need/require a wide range of/different communication strategies.*

3. *The implementation of this strategy by (world) governments may lead to reductions in pollution.*

4. *The recycling of waste may improve the chances of reducing poverty in the area / may lead to a reduction of poverty in the area / may lead to an improved chance of reducing poverty in the area.*

# Showing Balance in your Essay

The IELTS writing exam prepares you for writing within an academic and professional setting where you need to be respectful of others' ideas.

### Use cautious language.

In your essays, it would look awful if you said something like *'These people are completely wrong'* or *'I think these researchers were wrong.'* Instead, you would need to express yourself more diplomatically, for example: *'However, it might be the case that ....'* or *'Recent research suggests that this is not the case.'*

You are supposed to analyse different sides and project a sense of impartiality while you say whether you agree or disagree.

Remember, you always need to remain modest about your opinion and show the reader that you understand that you may be wrong, just like anybody else.

For example:

*"Students have a very low level of basic mathematical knowledge due to over-dependence on calculators."*

This is the student's personal opinion, but she/he cannot write this without evidence. In the IELTS exam, you are not likely going to be able to cite real evidence to support your

Master IELTS Writing Band 9 Essays

arguments, so you need to change your language: *"Over-dependence on calculators* **may** *have a negative effect on the basic mathematical knowledge of* **some students."**

This is also called 'hedging' language because 'to hedge against something' means to protect yourself from its negative consequences.

Students often make the mistake of using cautious language where it is not appropriate. They sometimes use *'would,' 'might,' 'likely to,'* etc., because they have learnt that these verbs are common in academic writing.

For example:

*"Annual financial reports* **might** *include information from financial statements and other sources."*

You don´t need to know a lot about accounting or business to understand that the objective of financial reports is to provide financial information taken from financial statements and other sources. Therefore, the verb *'might'* can´t be used here.

## Remember...

### Link your sentences in formal writing

Always use Linking Adverbs like *therefore, additionally, consequently, firstly, secondly, finally, moreover, however*

37

## Use synonyms to replace basic level vocabulary

To (purpose)= *in order to, so as to*

Like = *such as, for example, for instance*

Get = *receive, acquire, obtain*

Help = *aid, assist, support*

## Not only does X do Y, but it also does Z

Look at the difference between these sentences...

**Version 1:** *Working gives you the experience to help your career prospects. Working also improves essential skills like social skills.*

**Version 2:** *Not only does working provide you with experience to help your career prospects, but it also improves essential skills such as social interaction and communication.*

# Focus on the Topic and the Task

Task 2 in the IELTS writing exam is essential if you want to get a high band score in the exam. It is easy to considerably improve your writing score as long as you are prepared to take some advice and practice, practice, practice.

Essay instructions have two parts. You must understand both the topic and the task before you start the essay.

**The first part tells you the topic of the essay:**

*Some people believe that more funds should be invested into space exploration as it is a vital form of investigation for the future of humanity, while others believe it is a waste of vital funding that could otherwise be used towards more essential projects here on earth.*

*OR*

*Space exploration is much too expensive, and the money should be spent on more important things.*

*OR*

*Despite the availability of numerous gyms, many people are living more sedentary lifestyles.*

**The second part of the question gives you the specific task you must complete to get marks:**

Advantages & Disadvantages with your opinion: *Discuss both these views and give your own opinion.*

39

*Or*

Only your opinion essay: *What is your opinion?*

*Or*

Problem essay: *What problems are associated with this?*

*What solutions can you suggest?*

# Common Mistakes in the IELTS Essay

**<u>Don't use (...) or (etc.) when you are writing lists.</u>**

**It looks lazy in an essay.**

- Write lists like this; (A and B), (A, B, and C), or (A, B, C, and D).

- Example: "Some of the biggest issues humanity faces at the moment are pollution, poverty, disease, and global warming."

**<u>Don't use question marks in your essay:</u>**

- Don't ask the reader any questions in your essays.

  For example;

- "What is the best way to reduce pollution in developing countries?"-

**<u>Don't use exclamation marks!!!!!!!!!!</u>**

For example, "It is probably true to say that, on the whole, we use too much plastic!"

## Use Formal English

- Use "an increasing number of" (countable) or "an increasing amount of" (uncountable) to mean "more."

- Instead of writing "more businesses are paying attention to climate and sustainability issues," you could use "an increasing number of."

- For example: "an increasing number of businesses are paying attention to climate and sustainability issues." instead of "more businesses...."

- Add "significantly more" to express "a lot more" or "significant" to mean "quite a lot."

- Example: "significantly more businesses are paying attention to climate and sustainability issues." instead of "quite a lot more businesses ..."

- "a significant number of businesses are paying attention to climate and sustainability issues." OR "a sizeable number of businesses are paying attention to climate and sustainability issues." instead of "quite a lot of businesses..., or "a lot of businesses...."

- Use "a growing number of" (countable) or "growing amount of" (uncountable) to mean "more and more."

- Example: "a growing number of businesses are paying attention to climate and sustainability issues."

# Master IELTS Writing Band 9 Essays

## Avoid Contractions

- Avoid contractions in your essay!

    Examples:

- wouldn't = would not

- couldn't = could not

- mightn't = might not

- Etc.

## "But," "And" & "Because"

- Avoid starting a sentence with "But" or "And."

- Use "Furthermore,...", "In addition,..." instead of "And."

- Use "However,..." instead of "But."

- Use "Since...", "As a result,..." instead of "Because..."

- There are instances when we can start a formal or semi-formal sentence with "Because," but the options above are better.

43

## "Most" & "Almost"

- "Most" = adjective meaning the largest quantity, amount, degree, or number of....

- Followed by a noun, prepositional phrase, or adjective

- "Most proponents of...."

- "the most beneficial solution...."

- "in most cases...."

- "most of my peers...."

- "Almost" = adverb meaning nearly, not completely.

- "There are almost 700 million people living in extreme poverty, according to the World Bank."

- "Almost 10% of the world's population lives in extreme poverty, according to the World Bank."


## Rookie Errors

- Articles (a, an, no article)

- Subject-Verb Agreement

- Singular-Plural

- Countable/Uncountable Nouns

*Master IELTS Writing Band 9 Essays*

\* Learn how to use them in English and pay close attention when you are writing.

**\* Review the Rookie Errors Module in the Advanced IELTS Writing Course.**

## Here is a special discount for the course on
### ©Udemy https://bit.ly/3OF0v0h

## <u>Avoid Personal Opinions in Body Paragraphs</u>

- **Only for Introduction or conclusion (usually):**

"I think"

"I believe"

"in my opinion"

- This is a general rule and does not mean you will automatically lose marks if you break it.

- However, you should definitely follow it to keep your essay well-structured.

- Use impersonal opinions in the body paragraphs

"Some people believe that…. "

"Others argue that…. "

"There are those who claim that…."

"It is probably true to say that…. "

"Nobody would dispute the fact that…"

### **A Global Perspective**

- Essay questions are asked from a global perspective

- Avoid relating the essay question only to your country unless the question tells you to do so.

- Use your personal experiences, but present them with a global perspective. You can do this by generalizing ideas, reactions, opinions, and experiences with language like *'Many people…', 'A large number of people/users/customers/holiday/makers, etc.'*

  For example: instead of *"Factories in my city release toxic waste into the river, but the government does nothing to stop them"*…

  Write: *"Factories across the world release toxic waste into water supplies, but many governments are unable to stop them.."*

### **Use linking words**

- Start body paragraphs and conclusion with linking words and transition phrases.

- Keep your sentences short and well-linked.

- You will get marks for organization if you do this right.

For example

- Firstly,… Secondly,… Thirdly,…

- On the one hand,…. On the other hand,…

- To sum up, …

## **Personal Pronouns**

Avoid using personal pronouns in the body paragraphs of your essay if possible.

You should delete or rephrase:

*Me, you, I, we, us,*

You can rephrase it as:

*Workers, inhabitants, businesses, young people, students, people, society, etc.*

For example:

Instead of: "If I study at university, I will have more career opportunities."

# Marc Roche

Write: "If people/young people/students study at university, they will have more career opportunities."

## **Be Realistic in Your Language**

- Unless you are presenting a 100% fact like *"Water begins to boil at 100°C"* …

- Make sure your sentences show that you understand that what you say is not always true in every case!

- Avoid using words like;

- *all / every / none / only / always / never / totally / completely*

- Be careful with this language!

- For example: "When people start a new job they feel anxious…."

- Should be: "Many people feel anxious when they start a new job…."

- "All students need help with accommodation when they start at university."

- Should be: "A large number of (Many) students need help with accommodation when they start at university."

48

# Master IELTS Writing Band 9 Essays

## Avoid Using "Thing"

For example

- Instead of "When students get their first job, they are able to learn many new things."

- Write, "When students get their first job, they are able to learn many new skills, such as time- management, interpersonal communication, and goal-setting."

- You are avoiding the word "thing," which is vague, and you are giving specific examples.

# How to Evaluate Your IELTS Writing

The following table gives you a glimpse of what examiners are asking themselves when they read your writing test and decide on your score.

| Task achievement | Did you understand and answer the question? Is there a clear opinion? What information did you include? Are there at least 150 (Task 1) or 250 words (Task 2)? |
|---|---|
| Organisation | How well did you plan and organise the writing task? Did you use good connecting words? |
| Vocabulary | What vocabulary did you use? Did you use it well? How good is the spelling? To get a high band score, you must: Have a good range of vocabulary used correctly. Attempts to use less common vocabulary and uses it correctly a lot of the time. Very few or no spelling mistakes |
| Grammar | What grammar did you use? Did you use it well? How good is the punctuation? |

# Master IELTS Writing Band 9 Essays

|  | To get a high band score, you must: |
|  | Produce a lot of error-free sentences. |
|  | Use a variety of complex sentences and have good control of grammar |
|  | Have good control of punctuation |

# Brainstorming and Planning Recap

- You must write at least the number of words specified, or you will lose marks.

- You will not have time to count words in the exam, so count words when you are practicing so you know roughly how to write.

- It is essential to generate ideas as quickly as possible.

- Use mind-maps, spider-grams, and lists to organise information quickly.

- A good essay must have a beginning, middle, and end.

- Decide what you are going to write and make a brief plan outlining what each paragraph will contain.

- Write brief notes on what you want to include in each paragraph. This helps to prompt you to write your essay and serves as a useful checklist when you have finished.

- A useful guide to follow is to write approximately 50 words in your introduction paragraph, around 170 words or more in your main body paragraphs, and 30-40 words in your conclusion. Remember that these numbers are flexible.

# The Five Main Types of IELTS Essay

- Opinion Essay (Agree or Disagree)

- Advantages & Disadvantages Essay

- Problem & Solution Essay

- Discussion Essay

- Two-part Essay Question

# Opinion Essays

# Master IELTS Writing Band 9 Essays

# Two Types of Opinion Essay Question:

There are two main types of Opinion Essay in the IELTS test:

**Type 1:** Opinion essays where the exam question gives you both sides of an argument.

**Type 2:** Opinion essays where only one side is presented in the question.

## Type 1: Both sides given in the question

**Typical end question(s):**

- "What is your opinion?"

**Full Question Example:**

*Some people believe that violence on TV, in films, and in computer games has a damaging effect on society. Others deny that these factors have any significant influence on people's behavior. What is your opinion?*

## Marc Roche

**Tactics:**

You can…

- Agree 100% with one side

- Partly Agree with one side

# Type 2: One side given in the question

**Typical end question(s):**

- "Do you agree?"

- or "What is your opinion?"

- or "To what extent do you agree?"

**Full Question Example:**

*Some people believe that violence on TV, in films, and in computer games has a damaging effect on society. What is your opinion?*

**Tactics:**

You can…

- Agree 100%

# Master IELTS Writing Band 9 Essays

- Disagree 100%

- Partly Agree

# How to Agree 100% with One Side

In the example below, we will look at a Type 2 question that only gives one side of the argument. However, you can use the following approach for both types of questions, so don't worry □

### <u>Example Question:</u>

*According to some people, students from all economic backgrounds should be able to attend university. They believe that the government should provide free university education for everyone.*

*Do you agree with this view?*

In other words…. The above question is asking you:

*Do you agree that the government should provide free university for everyone?*

- You need to decide whether you think that university education should be paid for by the students (disagree), …or whether you think it should be paid for by the government (agree).

- Then, give reasons why.

- In our example response, we are going to say, "agree."

## Planning & Brainstorming Process:

### About the Planning Process:

1. It's CRUCIAL to have your paragraph ideas and supporting reasons planned in note form BEFORE you start writing.

- Students who don't do this, often get confused and have to rewrite sections of their essays.

- They lose marks for having a disorganized, unclear essay

- Or they lose marks for running out of time and not finishing their essay

2. When you have your ideas and your supporting reasons for each idea, your essay will be MUCH easier to write!

- You will feel less stressed and have a more clear focus.

*Master IELTS Writing Band 9 Essays*

- Therefore, you will likely get better grades in the exam.

**Note-taking During Planning:**

The following is a simulation of the notes you could make while you are planning your essay.

## Notes:

Question: *Do you agree that the government should provide free university for everyone?*

Answer: *Yes.*

*Because....*

## Reasons:

Reason 1: *Without financial support, many students who want to go to university have no other way to fulfill their dreams, + those who work and study will have worse results.*

Reason 2: *Educating the population is a long-term investment into the future of any country. No country can prosper without an educated population.*

## Detailed notes for Reasons 1 and 2:

*1. Without financial support, many students who want to go to university have no other way to fulfill their dreams, + those who work and study will have worse results.*

- *Many learners are unable to pay for their university education, even though they really want degrees.*

- *Even when students can afford to pay for university, they often have to take out loans and work part-time to pay for their living costs.*

- *This can severely affect grades and future career development.*

- *It can also leave them with large debts to pay when they finish studying.*

*2. Educating the population is a long-term investment into the future of any country. No country can prosper without an educated population.*

- *For example, taxpayers' money is misused by the government on initiatives like space exploration.*

- *If a country can't educate its population, there is no sense in investing large amounts of money into ambitious space projects.*

- *A more sensible distribution of government funds could allow many students to fulfill their dreams.*

- *More educated society, which would benefit the country as a whole for many years (to come).*

## Master IELTS Writing Band 9 Essays

**IELTS Essay Planning Tips Summary (One-sided Opinion Essay)**

1. Find the main opinion expressed in the essay question.

2. Decide if you agree or disagree.

3. Brainstorm main points

4. Short notes about supporting reasons

# Introduction

In the following section, we are going to look at how you can write the introduction part of your IELTS essay. If you follow these steps and practice regularly before the exam, you will find great success.

Exam Question:

*According to some people, students from all economic backgrounds should be able to attend university. They believe that the government should provide free university education for everyone.*

*Do you agree with this view?*

### 1st - Paraphrase the Issue

The first thing you need to do is paraphrase the issue that the question is focusing on. Use synonyms, turns of phrase, and colocations to do this. Here is a good example of how you can change the sentence without losing its meaning and show the examiner that you have an excellent command of English:

Original sentence(s):

According to some people, students from all economic backgrounds should be able to attend university. They believe that the government should provide free university education for everyone.

Paraphrased Version:

*The question of whether or not the government should consider making <u>tertiary education</u> <u>freely available</u> to <u>all learners</u> has been the subject of recent/ heated public discussion/ debate.*

## What exactly have we changed?

"university education"

"tertiary education." These are essentially the same thing.

"provide free university education."

has become "make tertiary education freely available."

"Students from all economic backgrounds"

has become "all learners."

*We've also added the standard sentence structure:* **The question of whether or not ……………………… has been the subject of recent/heated public discussion.**

This structure is very useful so that we can comfortably paraphrase the issue.

## 2nd - Answer the Question

Original Question:

Do you agree with this view?

Answer:

*Higher education, in my opinion, should be free regardless of income, <u>based on the grounds that</u> it would benefit both individuals and society.*

**What synonyms have we used?**

In this part of our introduction, we've used another synonym for "university education," "higher education." Then, to add extra variety to our language, we've used "on the grounds that" instead of "because." We've then moved on to specifying *why* we think higher education should be free without being too specific (*it would benefit both individuals and society*).

So there you have it, that's all you need to do to write your introduction for the IELTS essay. Here is the full version of the paragraph we've just written together.

*The question of whether or not the government should consider making tertiary education freely available to all learners has been the subject of recent/heated public discussion/debate. Higher education, in my opinion, should be free regardless of income, based on the grounds that it would benefit both individuals and society.*

# Body Paragraph 1

In this paragraph, we are going to fully explain the first reason why we believe that university should be free for all learners.

Structure:

1- State One Reason or Argument

2- Expand/Explain

3- Example

This 1st sentence connects to the question and gives a reason why you agree.

*Firstly, one argument in favor of eliminating university fees is that there are many learners who are unable to pay for their education, despite their strong desire to obtain degrees.*

**What vocabulary have we used so far?**

*Firstly,*

This indicates to the examiner that we are listing our first argument.

*one argument in favor of...*

This connects our new paragraph back to the question and tells the examiner that we are going to give an argument in favour of free university education.

*eliminating university fees*

We are paraphrasing the issue with the verb "eliminating", as another way of saying that the government should provide free education for all students.

*unable to pay*

We are using "unable to pay", as a formal substitute for "can't pay." This shows the examiner that the writer knows and can use different options depending on the context they are writing in.

*their education*

We are using a more general synonym here to write about university education. Even though "education" is more general than "university education," "tertiary education," and "higher education," we don't need to specify this time, as we have already mentioned it clearly in the essay. Using some slightly more general terms once you've specified is a great way of adding variety to your writing and showing the examiner your command of English.

The rest of the paragraph explains why this is important. We will then give an example, adopting a 'world view,' before giving details of the negative consequences of not helping students.

Why this is important:

*Without sufficient financial support/backing, these students have no other way to fulfill their dreams.*

Give an example, adopting a 'world view':

*Even in cases where students can afford to pay for university, they often have to take out loans and work part-time to pay for their living costs.*

Give details of the negative consequences of not helping students:

*This can severely affect their grades, and therefore, their future career development. It can also leave them with large debts to pay when they finish studying. These financial barriers may discourage highly talented students from pursuing a university education.*

So, the entire first body paragraph would look like this:

**Firstly, one argument in favor of eliminating university fees is that there are many learners who are unable to pay for their education, despite their strong desire to obtain degrees. Without sufficient financial support, these students have no other way to fulfill their dreams. Even in cases where students can afford to pay for university, they often have to take out loans and work part-time to pay for their living costs. This can severely affect their grades, and therefore, their future career development. It can also leave them with large debts to pay when they finish studying. These financial barriers may discourage highly talented students from pursuing a university education.**

## Body Paragraph 2

Again, in this paragraph, we are going to fully explain the second reason why we believe that university should be free for all learners.

Structure:

1- State One Reason or Argument

2- Expand/Explain

3- Example

This 1st sentence connects to the question and gives a reason why you agree.

*Secondly, no country can prosper without an educated population, so funding free university education is a long-term investment into the future of the country.*

Give an example, adopting a 'world view' or a 'society-wide view':

*Taxpayers' money is arguably being misused by governments on initiatives like space exploration.*

# Master IELTS Writing Band 9 Essays

Give details of the negative consequences of not helping students AND the benefits of helping them:

*If a country can't educate its population, there is no sense in investing large amounts of money into ambitious space projects. A far more sensible distribution of government funds could allow thousands of students to fulfill their dreams. This would lead to a more educated society, which would, no doubt, benefit the country as a whole for many years (to come).*

So, the entire second body paragraph would look like this:

**Secondly, no country can prosper without an educated population, so funding free university education is a long-term investment into the future of the country. Taxpayers' money is arguably being misused by the government on initiatives like space exploration. If a country can't educate its population, there is no sense in investing large amounts of money into ambitious space projects. A far more sensible distribution of government funds could allow thousands of students to fulfill their dreams. This would lead to a more educated society, which would, no doubt, benefit the country as a whole for many years (to come).**

71

# Conclusion

In the conclusion part of your essay, you should give a summary of the main points you've mentioned and then restate your opinion so that you finish with a clear message.

**Conclusion**

1- Summary of Main Points

**2-** Restate opinion

Summary of main points:

*In conclusion, free university education, regardless of income, is crucial for any society seeking sustainable progress. Expensive tuition fees may discourage some individuals from pursuing university degrees, as young people are often unwilling to carry the burden of their loans for many years after graduation, making university less appealing.*

Restate opinion:

*The government should be responsible for the cost of tertiary education. Hence, it would be appropriate for the government to better distribute financial resources in order to do this.*

So the conclusion paragraph would be:

*In conclusion, free university education, regardless of income, is crucial for any society seeking sustainable progress. Expensive tuition fees may discourage some individuals from pursuing university degrees, as young people are often unwilling to carry the burden of their loans for many years after graduation, making university less appealing. The government should be responsible for the cost of tertiary education. Hence, it would be appropriate for the government to better distribute financial resources in order to do this.*

## Linking Words

1. Use linking words like *firstly, secondly, thirdly, etc*. They are relatively simple and make it easier for the examiner to follow the development of your ideas.

You can use them to separate paragraphs like in the example above, or you can use them to separate reasons (evidence) within the same paragraphs like we've done in the example below:

*Several studies have proven that global warming is already having a negative impact on human life. Firstly, it has been shown to affect crops worldwide, leading to significant shortages in some cases. Secondly, global temperature increases have compromised food production in some regions, which has caused inflation and a deterioration of the quality of life of the people affected. Thirdly, it is causing unnecessary stress, and in some cases conflict, within already vulnerable sectors of the world population.*

# Repetition

**Repetition** can be good sometimes if you do it for a good reason.

- Using repetition, you improve comprehension.

- You can use synonyms to repeat important parts of your ideas.

- The examiner can't read your mind, so repeating yourself sometimes reminds the examiner about what you are talking about!

Check out the example below to see how you can use repetition to create a strong paragraph.

*Several studies have proven that global warming is already having a negative impact on human life. Firstly, it has been shown to affect crops worldwide, leading to significant shortages in some cases. Secondly, global temperature increases have compromised food production in some regions, which has caused inflation and a deterioration of the quality of life of the people affected. Thirdly, rising temperatures are causing unnecessary stress, and in some cases conflict, within already vulnerable sectors of the world population.*

## Special Vocabulary

- *Tertiary education, higher education, university education*

- *Income- money you receive*

- *Sufficient - enough*

- *Financial support - funding*

- *Government funds - Government funding - Government money - Government resources*

- *Fulfill – reach (ambitions, dreams, etc.)*

- *, no doubt - undoubtedly*

- *Years to come- years in the future*

- *Sustainable progress- healthy growth*

- *Discourage X from –ing - stop X from -ing*

- *(are) unwilling to- don't want to*

- *Carry the burden of – take on the responsibility of*

- *Less appealing - Less attractive*

- *Hence, - Therefore,*

Master IELTS Writing Band 9 Essays

# Notes Section

## Revision Exercise

Fill the gaps with an appropriate word or phrase from the box:

| | | | |
|---|---|---|---|
| *The question of whether or not* | *in my opinion* | *is arguably* | *Secondly,* |
| *These financial barriers* | *Without sufficient financial support* | *Firstly, one argument in favor of eliminating university fees is that* | *misused* |
| *Even in cases* | *any society seeking sustainable progress* | *may discourage* | *tertiary education* |
| *In conclusion,* | *unwilling to* | *burden* | *severely* |
| *, no doubt,* | *funding* | *lead to* | *pursuing* |

# Master IELTS Writing Band 9 Essays

## Model Essay

According to some people, students from all economic backgrounds should be able to attend university. They believe that the government should provide free university education for everyone.

Do you agree with this view?

.......................... *the government should consider making tertiary education available to all learners has been the subject of recent public discussion. Higher education, ................, should be free regardless of income, based on the grounds that it would benefit both individuals and society.*

........................................................ .............................................. *there are many learners who are unable to pay for their education, despite their strong desire to obtain degrees. ..............................., these students have no other way to fulfill their dreams. ................. where students can afford to pay for university, they often have to take out loans and work part-time to pay for their living costs. This can ................. affect their grades, and therefore, their future career development. It can also leave them with large debts to pay when they finish studying.*

........................ *may discourage highly talented students from pursuing a university education.*

.................. *no country can prosper without an educated population, so ............ free university education is a long-term investment into the future of the country. Taxpayers' money ........ ............ being ............. by governments on initiatives like space exploration. If a country can't educate its population, there is no sense in investing large amounts of money into ambitious space projects. A far more sensible distribution of government funds could allow thousands of students to fulfill their dreams. This would ............. a more educated society, which would ............. benefit the country as a whole for many years (to come).*

.................., *free university education, regardless of income, is crucial for ............................................ Expensive tuition fees .................... some individuals from ............... university degrees, as young people are often ................... carry the .......... of their loans for many years after graduation, making university less appealing. The government should be responsible for the cost of ....................... Hence, it would be appropriate for the government to better distribute financial resources in order to do this.*

# Master IELTS Writing Band 9 Essays

## Answers: Full Sample Essay

According to some people, students from all economic backgrounds should be able to attend university. They believe that the government should provide free university education for everyone.

Do you agree with this view?

*The question of whether or not the government should consider making tertiary education available to all learners has been the subject of recent public discussion. Higher education, in my opinion, should be free regardless of income, based on the grounds that it would benefit both individuals and society.*

*Firstly, one argument in favor of eliminating university fees is that there are many learners who are unable to pay for their education, despite their strong desire to obtain degrees. Without sufficient financial support, these students have no other way to fulfill their dreams. Even in cases where students can afford to pay for university, they often have to take out loans and work part-time to pay for their living costs. This can severely affect their grades, and therefore, their future career development. It can also leave them with large debts to pay when they finish studying. These financial barriers may discourage highly talented students from pursuing a university education.*

*Secondly, no country can prosper without an educated population, so funding free university education is a long-term investment into the future of the country. Taxpayers' money is arguably being misused by governments on initiatives like space exploration. If a country can't educate its population, there is no sense in investing large amounts of money into ambitious space projects. A far more sensible distribution of government funds could allow thousands of students to fulfill their dreams. This would lead to a more educated society, which would, no doubt, benefit the country as a whole for many years (to come).*

*In conclusion, free university education, regardless of income, is crucial for any society seeking sustainable progress. Expensive tuition fees may discourage some individuals from pursuing university degrees, as young people are often unwilling to carry the burden of their loans for many years after graduation, making university less appealing. The government should be responsible for the cost of tertiary education. Hence, it would be appropriate for the government to better distribute financial resources in order to do this.*

*Master IELTS Writing Band 9 Essays*

# How to Give a Balanced Opinion Essay
# (Taking ideas from Both Sides)

- This style of essay takes ideas from both sides of the issue.

- Doesn't completely agree with both sides but agrees with SOME aspects of both arguments.

- Doesn't discuss both sides robotically but instead expresses a CLEAR opinion based on logic.

## Balanced Opinion Essay Example

*Certain people truly believe that planning for the future is a complete waste of time. They think that the present should be the main focus.*

*Do you agree with this view?*

# Introduction

## 1. Paraphrase:

*Some people think that living for the moment and enjoying the present is more important than making plans for the future.*

## 2. Give Clear Opinion

*In my opinion, a life without any planning for the future can be chaotic and stressful. So while it is important to be present and enjoy the moment, a degree of planning is always required in order to live a full, happy life.*

So, the introduction would look like this:

*Some people think that living for the moment and enjoying the present is more important than making plans for the future. In my opinion, a life without any planning for the future can be chaotic and stressful. So while it is important to be present and enjoy the moment, a degree of planning is always required in order to live a full, happy life.*

# Body Paragraphs

- ALWAYS plan your body paragraphs

- DO NOT get distracted and go deep into discussing advantages and disadvantages

Quick Plan:

Body Paragraph 1: Stress and physical health

Body Paragraph 2: Motivation + life or career goals

Body Paragraph 3: Planning is compatible with focusing on the present. It's about balance!

## Body Paragraph 1 Plan

- People who have goals generally understand what they want in life and have more confidence in their decisions.

- Because of this, they are happier and more successful in many cases.

- Never knowing what you need to do next or constantly making mistakes and forgetting important things can be very stressful and affect your quality of life. It can also affect your long-term health.

## Body Paragraph 1 Example

*It is probably true to say that people who have goals generally understand what they want in life, and as a result, have more confidence in their decisions since they have usually thought them through and planned them. This leads to higher levels of long-term happiness and success in many cases. Never knowing what you need to do next or constantly making mistakes and forgetting important events can be highly stressful and severely affect your quality of life, as well as your long-term health.*

## Body Paragraph 2 Example

*Furthermore, making plans for the future provides people with motivation. In fact, most individuals are motivated by a vision they have for their future. Making plans for the future renders a person's growth more feasible. It is true that even the most successful people can become distracted and discouraged at times. As a result, they may find it difficult to fully appreciate their accomplishments and enjoy their success. Having clearly defined goals can help minimize this issue.*

### Body Paragraph 3 Example

*Finally, a balanced lifestyle that includes specific and realistic goals, together with a healthy amount of focusing on the present, is more likely to lead to long-term happiness and fulfillment. There is evidence that suggests that purposefully focusing on the present can be part of a healthy, balanced lifestyle. Practices such as mindfulness and meditation, for instance, have numerous reported benefits, such as reducing stress and even blood pressure.*

## Conclusion

*In conclusion, I believe that developing a long-term strategy and concentrating on the present are not mutually exclusive. Concentrating on clear goals helps individuals to become more organized in their daily lives and happier overall. As a result, it would be better if people started planning for their futures as soon as possible, but without neglecting their short-term happiness and wellbeing.*

## Balanced Opinion Essay Recap

- Clearly written opinion in the Introduction section

- Does not contradict itself

- Body paragraphs explain the opinion in more detail and give clear reasons for the opinion

# Master IELTS Writing Band 9 Essays

## Revision Exercise

Fill the gaps with an appropriate word or phrase from the box:

| | | | |
|---|---|---|---|
| *There is evidence that suggests that* | *long-term* | *Furthermore,* | *There are numerous reasons* |
| *In fact,* | *Finally,* | *feasible* | *highly* |
| *fully appreciate* | | *are not mutually exclusive* | *discouraged* |
| *and as a result,* | *can be* | *It is probably true to say that* | *renders* |
| *short-term* | *Some people think that* | *for instance,* | *This leads to* |

89

## Marc Roche

### Model Essay

**Certain people truly believe that planning for the future is a complete waste of time. They think that the present should be the main focus.**

**Do you agree with this view?**

........................... *living for the moment and enjoying the present is more important than making plans for the future. In my opinion, a life without any planning for the future ............... chaotic and stressful. So while it is important to be present and enjoy the moment, a degree of planning is always required in order to live a full, happy life.*
*.................................. to make plans for the future.*

*............................................. people who have goals generally understand what they want in life, ............................. have more confidence in their decisions since they have usually thought them through and planned them. ..................... higher levels of ................... happiness and success in many cases. Never knowing what you need to do next or constantly making mistakes and forgetting important*

# Master IELTS Writing Band 9 Essays

events can be ................... *stressful and severely affect your quality of life, as well as your long-term health.*

........................ *making plans for the future provides people with motivation.* ............ *most individuals are motivated by a vision they have for their future. Making plans for the future* ................... *a person's growth more* ................... *It is true that even the most successful people can become distracted and* ............................ *at times. As a result, they may find it difficult to* ................... *their accomplishments and enjoy their success. Having clearly defined goals can help minimize this issue.*

....................... *a balanced lifestyle that includes specific and realistic goals, together with a healthy amount of focusing on the present, is more likely to lead to long-term happiness and fulfillment.*

......................................................................

*purposefully focusing on the present can be part of a healthy, balanced lifestyle. Practices such as mindfulness and meditation,* .................................. *have numerous reported benefits, such as reducing stress and even blood pressure.*

In conclusion, *I believe that developing a long-term strategy and concentrating on the present* ........................................ *Concentrating on clear goals helps individuals to become more organized in their daily lives and happier overall. As a result, it would be better if people started planning for their futures as soon as possible, but without neglecting their ................. happiness and wellbeing.*

# Answers: Full Sample Essay

**Certain people truly believe that planning for the future is a complete waste of time. They think that the present should be the main focus.**

**Do you agree with this view?**

*Some people think that living for the moment and enjoying the present is more important than making plans for the future. In my opinion, a life without any planning for the future can be chaotic and stressful. So while it is important to be present and enjoy the moment, a degree of planning is always required in order to live a full, happy life. There are numerous reasons to make plans for the future.*

*It is probably true to say that people who have goals generally understand what they want in life, and as a result, have more confidence in their decisions since they have usually thought them through and planned them. This leads to higher levels of long-term happiness and success in many cases. Never knowing what you need to do next or constantly making mistakes and forgetting important events can be highly stressful and severely affect your quality of life, as well as your long-term health.*

Furthermore, making plans for the future provides people with motivation. In fact, most individuals are motivated by a vision they have for their future. Making plans for the future renders a person's growth more feasible. It is true that even the most successful people can become distracted and discouraged at times. As a result, they may find it difficult to fully appreciate their accomplishments and enjoy their success. Having clearly defined goals can help minimize this issue.

Finally, a balanced lifestyle that includes specific and realistic goals, together with a healthy amount of focusing on the present, is more likely to lead to long-term happiness and fulfillment. There is evidence that suggests that purposefully focusing on the present can be part of a healthy, balanced lifestyle. Practices such as mindfulness and meditation, for instance, have numerous reported benefits, such as reducing stress and even blood pressure.

In conclusion, I believe that developing a long-term strategy and concentrating on the present are not mutually exclusive. Concentrating on clear goals helps individuals to become more organized in their daily lives and happier overall. As a result, it would be better if people started planning for their futures as soon as possible, but without neglecting their short-term happiness and wellbeing.

# Advantages & Disadvantages Essay

## Types of Question

There are two main types of 'IELTS advantages and disadvantages' essay questions:

**Type 1:** Questions that ask for your opinion.

**Type 2:** Questions that do not require you to state your opinion.

## Typical Question Words

### <u>Advantages & Disadvantages Essay with Opinion</u>

"Do the benefits outweigh the drawbacks?"

"Do the advantages outweigh the disadvantages?"

"What are the advantages and disadvantages of....?"

"Discuss the advantages and disadvantages. Give your opinion."

**Example:**

*A lot of countries rely on tourism as a main source of income. However, tourism can also cause problems if it is not managed correctly.*

*Describe the advantages and disadvantages of international tourism in today's modern world. Do you believe that the benefits of tourism outweigh its drawbacks?*

# Master IELTS Writing Band 9 Essays

<u>You should:</u>

Write about **+** and **−** and say if it's mostly positive or negative based on your analysis.

## **Advantages & Disadvantages Essay WITHOUT Opinion**

"Discuss the advantages and disadvantages."

"Discuss the advantages and disadvantages."

### Example:

*A lot of countries rely on tourism as a main source of income. However, tourism can also cause problems if it is not managed correctly.*

*Discuss the advantages and disadvantages of tourism in the modern world.*

<u>You should:</u>

Write about **+** and **−**

## Full Task Example

*When individuals with cultural differences work and live together, they are said to be living in a multi-cultural society.*

*Do you believe that the advantages of living in a multi-cultural society outweigh the disadvantages?*

This question is asking for your opinion

## How to Brainstorm Ideas

### Advantages of Multi-Cultural Society

- Allows people to broaden their understanding of the world - more tolerance and improved relations among communities.

- Can give a place a unique mix, which adds to its identity.

- Can boost the local economy, providing jobs and prosperity.

### Disadvantages of Multi-Cultural Society

- Can lead to conflict and resentment if not managed properly.

# Master IELTS Writing Band 9 Essays

### Notes on Tactics

We need to pick a side and be tactical in our response to this question. We might not be able to explain the disadvantage we came up with properly in such a short essay since the issue is very complex. Therefore, we are going to say that the advantages outweigh the disadvantages, and we are going to treat this disadvantage superficially to save space and time. It's too complex to explain fully in a short paragraph.

## General Structure

### Introduction

1- Paraphrase Question

2- State Opinion

### Main Body Paragraph 1

1- State One Advantage

2- Expand/Explain

3- Example

### Main Body Paragraph 2

1- State One Advantage

99

2- Expand/Explain

3- Example

## Main Body Paragraph 3

1- State One Disadvantage

2- Expand/Explain

3- Example

## Conclusion

1- Summary of Main Points

2- Restate opinion

# Introduction

Essay Question:

*When individuals with cultural differences work and live together, they are said to be living in a multi-cultural society.*

*Do you believe that the advantages of living in a multi-cultural society outweigh the disadvantages?*

## 1st - Paraphrase the Issue

*The question of whether the benefits of living in a multi-cultural society outweigh its drawbacks has been sparking debate for several years.*

## 2nd - Answer the Question

*I believe that having individuals with different cultural backgrounds work and live together is beneficial on many levels and that, therefore, the advantages clearly outweigh the disadvantages.*

Therefore, this is what the introduction paragraph looks like...

*The question of whether the benefits of living in a multi-cultural society outweigh the drawbacks has been sparking debate for several years. I believe that having individuals with different cultural backgrounds work and live together is beneficial on many levels and that, therefore, the advantages clearly outweigh the disadvantages.*

## Body Paragraph 1

1- State One Advantages

2- Expand/Explain

3- Example

As we saw in the Opinion Essay, the first sentence connects to the topic of the question and signals to the reader what we are going to discuss. The first sentence, in this case, connects to the question and signals to the reader that we are going to talk about advantages.

*A variety of advantages are created by living and working in a diverse society.*

The rest explains the advantage(s)…

*For starters, multi-cultural environments allow people to broaden their understanding of the world and of human nature. Different cultures produce different perspectives and ideas, which help people learn more about the world. Having people from different parts of the world living together in the same region can provide excellent learning opportunities, as people are exposed to a variety of languages, cultures, and traditions. People can experience different foods, and different customs every day, leading to more tolerance and improved relations among communities.*

This is what the introduction paragraph looks like...

*A variety of advantages are created by living and working in a diverse society. For starters, multi-cultural environments allow people to broaden their understanding of the world and of human nature. Different cultures produce different perspectives and ideas, which help people learn more about the world. Having people from different parts of the world living together in the same region can provide excellent learning opportunities, as people are exposed to a variety of languages, cultures, and traditions. People can experience different foods, and different customs every day, leading to more tolerance and improved relations among communities.*

## Body Paragraph 2

1- State One Advantage

2- Expand/Explain

3- Example

We are going to signal to the reader that we will state another advantage in this paragraph:

*Furthermore, individuals from a variety of cultural backgrounds benefit society in many other ways.*

We will use an example to expand and explain this advantage:

*Because of their multi-cultural nature, countries like Australia, the UK, and Canada run a variety of yearly events to celebrate the coming together of different cultures.*

We now expand on and explain the advantage:

*These festivals serve as tourist attractions that boost the local economy, providing jobs and prosperity. These celebrations have the added effect of solidifying the area's identity and uniting people in celebration, which arguably contributes to a healthier, happier society.*

As you can see, it doesn't matter which order you choose with the example and explanation. You can use your example to expand and explain, or you can expand and explain and then include an example to support your claims.

So the whole paragraph would look like this

*Furthermore, individuals from a variety of cultural backgrounds benefit society in many other ways. Because of their multi-cultural nature, countries like Australia, the UK, and Canada run a variety of yearly events to celebrate the coming together of different cultures. These festivals serve as tourist attractions that boost the local economy, providing jobs and prosperity. These celebrations have the added effect of solidifying the area's identity and uniting people in celebration, which arguably contributes to a healthier, happier society.*

## Body Paragraph 3

First, we are going to signal to the reader that we will be talking about a disadvantage here. So, language like "one potential stumbling block, is…" is very useful. As soon as we've done this, we will state exactly what that disadvantage is, so we're not wasting too many words.

*One potential stumbling block is if the situation is not managed correctly and new communities do not become integrated.*

Now that we've stated our disadvantage, we will expand and explain a bit:

*This can lead to a feeling of isolation which often causes conflict and resentment if not managed properly.*

We will now give what could be considered as an example, even though we are keeping it very general in this case. We will finish the example by explaining the disadvantage in a little more detail, by being more specific.

*Furthermore, if communities become entrenched in specific areas within a city, and there are insufficient resources to serve all communities equally, this can result in further conflict, as a feeling of injustice becomes widespread.*

The full body paragraph would be:

**One potential stumbling block is if the situation is not managed correctly and new communities do not become integrated. This can lead to a feeling of isolation which often causes conflict and resentment if not managed properly. Furthermore, if communities become entrenched in specific areas within a city, and there are insufficient resources to serve all communities equally, this can result in further conflict, as a feeling of injustice becomes widespread.**

## Conclusion

First, we are going to summarise the main points.

*After taking into consideration all of the points made above, I do not see any significant disadvantages to living in a multi-cultural environment, provided the situation is managed correctly, and all communities are fully integrated.*

Next, we restate opinions.

*I am confident that, in theory, the advantages clearly outweigh the disadvantages from both an economic and a cultural standpoint. Furthermore, I believe that in order to develop as a society and prosper in the long term, we must foster an atmosphere of respect and tolerance among cultures. Cultural diversity can enrich society on many levels and force us to confront our prejudices.*

So the full conclusion would be

*After taking into consideration all of the points made above, I do not see any significant disadvantages to living in a multi-cultural environment, provided the situation is managed correctly, and all communities are fully integrated. I am confident that, in theory, the advantages clearly outweigh the disadvantages from both an economic and a cultural standpoint. Furthermore, I believe that in order to develop as a society and prosper in the long term, we must foster an atmosphere of respect and tolerance among cultures. Cultural diversity can enrich society on many levels and force us to confront our prejudices.*

## Quick Check

- Short and Sweet- To the point

- Effective paraphrase of the question in Introduction

- Clear opinion in Introduction

- Consistent opinion through the whole essay

- Each body paragraph explains advantage or disadvantage + gives well-explained, logical examples where necessary.

- Conclusion summarises opinion

# Linking Words

- **Use linking words like *"Furthermore,"* etc. These are quite straightforward and make it easier for the examiner to follow the development of your ideas.**

- **You can use them to separate paragraphs like in the example above, or you can use them to separate reasons (evidence) within the same paragraphs.**

- **Use synonyms to avoid excessive repetition:**

  *Furthermore, individuals from a variety of cultural backgrounds benefit society in many other ways. Because of their multi-cultural nature, countries like Australia, the UK, and Canada run a variety of festivals to celebrate the coming together of different cultures. These festivals* **serve as** *tourist attractions that boost the local economy, providing jobs and prosperity.* *These celebrations* *have the added effect of solidifying the area's identity and uniting people in celebration, which arguably contributes to a healthier, happier society.*

## Special Vocabulary

*Celebrations= Festivals= Street parties= Yearly events* (these are not perfect synonyms, but can be used as synonyms when we are discussing festivals and celebrations in general)

*Diverse= varied*

*Because of their multi-cultural nature,*

*Boost= enrich= improve*

*Solidify= consolidate= reinforce*

*Potential stumbling block= potential issue= possible problem*

*There are insufficient= there are not enough= there is a shortage of*

*(feeling of injustice) becomes widespread= feeling of injustice grows*

*from both an economic and a cultural standpoint= economically and culturally*

*we must foster= we must encourage*

*Cultural diversity can enrich society on many levels= Multiculturalism can improve society in many ways*

# Master IELTS Writing Band 9 Essays

## Notes Section

# Revision Exercise

Fill the gaps with an appropriate word or phrase from the box:

| is beneficial on many levels | For starters, | are exposed | serve as |
|---|---|---|---|
| | diverse | , therefore, | standpoint |
| this can result in | This can lead to | run | has been sparking debate for several years |
| from both an | , in theory, | broaden | enrich |
| prosperity | The question of whether | Furthermore, | we must foster |

## Master IELTS Writing Band 9 Essays

### Model Essay

**When individuals with cultural differences work and live together, they are said to be living in a multi-cultural society.**

**Do you believe that the advantages of living in a multi-cultural society outweigh the disadvantages?**

......................... *the benefits of living in a multi-cultural society outweigh the drawbacks*

..................................... *I believe that having individuals with different cultural backgrounds work and live together* ................................. *and that*............... *the advantages clearly outweigh the disadvantages.*

*A variety of advantages are created by living and working in a* ............... *society.* ......................... *multi-cultural environments allow people to* ............... *their understanding of the world and of human nature. Different cultures produce different perspectives and ideas, which help people learn more about the world. Having people from different parts of the world living together in the same region can provide excellent learning opportunities, as people* ..................... *to a variety of languages, cultures, and traditions. People can experience different foods, and different customs every day, leading to more tolerance and improved relations among communities.*

*.......................... individuals from a variety of cultural backgrounds benefit society in many other ways. Because of their multi-cultural nature, countries like Australia, the UK, and Canada .................. a variety of yearly events to celebrate the coming together of different cultures. These festivals ................... tourist attractions that boost the local economy, providing jobs and ............. These celebrations have the added effect of solidifying the area's identity and uniting people in celebration, which arguably contributes to a healthier, happier society.*

*One potential stumbling block is if the situation is not managed correctly and new communities do not become integrated. ........................... a feeling of isolation which often causes conflict and resentment if not managed properly. Furthermore, if communities become entrenched in specific areas within a city, and there are insufficient resources to serve all communities equally, ........................... further conflict, as a feeling of injustice becomes widespread.*

*After taking into consideration all of the points made above, I do not see any significant disadvantages to living in a multi-cultural environment, provided the situation is managed correctly, and all communities are fully integrated. I am confident*

*that.............................. the advantages clearly outweigh the*

*disadvantages .......................... economic and a cultural*

*........................ Furthermore, I believe that in order to develop as*

*a society and prosper in the long term, .................... an atmosphere*

*of respect and tolerance among cultures. Cultural diversity can*

*....................society on many levels and force us to confront our*

*prejudices.*

## Answers: Full Sample Essay

When individuals with cultural differences work and live together, they are said to be living in a multi-cultural society.

Do you believe that the advantages of living in a multi-cultural society outweigh the disadvantages?

*The question of whether the benefits of living in a multi-cultural society outweigh the drawbacks has been sparking debate for several years. I believe that having individuals with different cultural backgrounds work and live together is beneficial on many levels and that, therefore, the advantages clearly outweigh the disadvantages.*

*A variety of advantages are created by living and working in a diverse society. For starters, multi-cultural environments allow people to broaden their understanding of the world and of human nature. Different cultures produce different perspectives and ideas, which help people learn more about the world. Having people from different parts of the world living together in the same region can provide excellent learning opportunities, as people are exposed to a variety of languages, cultures, and traditions. People can experience different foods, and different customs every day, leading to more tolerance and improved relations among communities.*

*Furthermore, individuals from a variety of cultural backgrounds benefit society in many other ways. Because of their multi-cultural nature, countries like Australia, the UK, and Canada run a variety of yearly events to celebrate the coming together of different cultures. These festivals serve as tourist attractions that boost the local economy, providing jobs and prosperity. These celebrations have the added effect of solidifying the area's identity and uniting people in celebration, which arguably contributes to a healthier, happier society.*

*One potential stumbling block is if the situation is not managed correctly and new communities do not become integrated. This can lead to a feeling of isolation which often causes conflict and resentment if not managed properly. Furthermore, if communities become entrenched in specific areas within a city, and there are insufficient resources to serve all communities equally, this can result in further conflict, as a feeling of injustice becomes widespread.*

*After taking into consideration all of the points made above, I do not see any significant disadvantages to living in a multi-cultural environment, provided the situation is managed correctly, and all communities are fully integrated. I am confident that, in theory, the advantages clearly outweigh the disadvantages from both an economic and a cultural standpoint. Furthermore, I believe that in order to develop as a society and prosper in the long term, we must foster an atmosphere of respect and tolerance among cultures. Cultural diversity can enrich society on many levels and force us to confront our prejudices.*

# Problem & Solution Essay

# 3 Types of Problem-Solution Essay

The three essay types:

- **Problem and solution**

- **Cause and solution**

- **Just the solution**

We will cover the most common type, which is problem-solution.

Cause- solution is exactly the same, but instead of analyzing the "problem," you analyze the "cause(s)" and then possible solutions.

It is very rare to get an essay where you only discuss solutions, but it is the easiest type: you focus 100% on solutions to the problem expressed in the question.

## Typical Question Phrases

Asking about the cause(s) or the problem(s):

*"What are some resulting issues, and how can they be addressed?"*

*"What problems can this cause, and how can they be addressed?"*

*"What issues arise from this, and how can we solve them?"*

# Master IELTS Writing Band 9 Essays

*"Why is this? How can it be solved?"*

*"What is the reason for this, and what measures can be taken to solve the issue?"*

Asking about the solution(s):

*"How can the problem be improved?"*

*"What measures could be introduced to solve this?"*

*"What solutions can be implemented to deal with the issue?"*

*"How can this issue be resolved/prevented?"*

## Full Task Example

*The number of people moving from rural to urban areas in search of a better life is increasing, but city life comes with its own set of issues.*

*What exactly are these issues, and how can they be solved?*

In this example, two questions have been phrased as one. What are the issues, and how can they be solved?

Issues and solutions = it's a problem-solution essay

# Two Typical General Structures

Both these structures would be the same length. It's up to you to choose the one you are most comfortable with.

### Typical Structure 1 for Problem-Solution Essay

- Introduction

- Body paragraph 1: Identify and explain 2-3 issues

- Body Paragraph 2: Explain the possible solutions

- Conclusion

### Typical Structure 2 for Problem-Solution Essay

- Introduction

- Body paragraph 1: Problem 1 + Solution

- Body paragraph 2: Problem 2 + Solution

- Body paragraph 3: Problem 3 + Solution

- Conclusion

Master IELTS Writing Band 9 Essays

## Common Mistakes

1. Using too many ideas.

2. Not writing enough detail about each idea.

3. Not linking problems and solutions.

4. Not being specific enough in explanations and examples, or not taking a world view on the issue.

# How To Understand Problem-Solution Essay Questions

**The first thing you need to do is analyse the question**

This is a crucial part of the planning process and will help you answer the question properly. This is CRUCIAL if you want to get an advanced grade (Bands 7-9).

### 1. General Topic words

Topic words describe the general subject of the question.

*The number **of people moving from rural to urban areas** in*

125

*search of a better life is increasing, but city life comes with its own set of* **issues.**

So, the question is about 'issues or problems' connected to 'city life.'

Many IELTS candidates write about causes here, but you don't have any time or space for this!

## 2. Instruction words

Instruction words tell you what specific ideas the examiner wants you to write about:

**What** *exactly* **are** *these* **issues,** *and* **how can** *they* **be solved?**

This question tells us that the examiner wants to read about issues (problems) and solutions.

# Brainstorming Ideas

- You need to come up with some ideas to write about.

- Write ideas as they come to your mind without worrying about high-level language or sounding amazing in English!

- Just write ideas as if you were having an informal chat with a family member or a friend.

- If you do it this way, you will come up with more ideas, as your brain won't be distracted by thinking about high-level vocabulary.

- Here are some ideas for the example essay question we looked at:

| Problems | Solutions |
|---|---|
| • Lots of people in the same space- Not enough housing<br><br>• Traffic<br><br>• Pollution + all its health risks | • Provide more affordable housing in city centers<br><br>• Better public transport<br><br>• Awareness campaigns + car-free zones like in London, Madrid, or Paris. |

# Introduction

Essay Question:

*The number of people moving from rural to urban areas in search of a better life is increasing, but city life comes with its own set of issues.*

*What exactly are these issues, and how can they be solved?*

### 1st - Paraphrase the Issue

*A growing number of people are relocating from rural to urban areas in search of a better quality of life.*

### 2nd – Give Some Details

*However, problems such as housing shortages, traffic congestion, and pollution can have a serious impact on that quality of life. This essay will examine these issues and propose potential solutions.*

So the whole introduction looks like this:

*A growing number of people are relocating from rural to urban areas in search of a better quality of life. However, problems such as housing shortages, traffic congestion, and pollution can have a serious impact on that quality of life. This essay will examine these issues and propose potential solutions.*

## Body Paragraph 1

The first issue + solution...

This 1st sentence connects to the question and signals what we are going to talk about.

***Firstly,*** *the dense concentration of people in cities has resulted in a shortage of affordable housing.*

2nd sentence gives a specific example or explains the problem in more detail.

*In several large cities, for example, a large number of people end up living in the suburbs since the shortage of space means renting in the city is too expensive.*

The 3rd and 4th sentences give solutions to the issue.

*As a first step, governments should provide more affordable housing in city centers. UK cities like Manchester and London, for example, have government housing near the city centers to assist low-income families.*

So the whole first body paragraph would be:

*Firstly, the dense concentration of people in cities has resulted in a shortage of affordable housing. In several large cities, for example, a large number of people end up living in the suburbs since the shortage of space means renting in the city is too expensive. As a first step, governments should provide more affordable housing in city centers. UK cities like Manchester and London, for example, have government housing near the city centers to assist low-income families.*

## Body Paragraph 2

The second issue + solution...

1st sentence connects the previous paragraph to this new paragraph and presents the new issue.

*Living far away from work forces people to commute on a daily basis, which contributes to the second issue, traffic congestion.*

We then use an example to offer a soli, realistic basis for our argument:

*Traffic congestion has become a critical issue in several cities worldwide. In Shanghai, for example, if you want to go from the East to the West, you may end up spending seven hours sitting in your car due to traffic jams.*

**Finally, we offer a solution, and then explain why this is an important issue and why it needs solving... ('because it affects the quality of life')**

*Something governments must improve, is transportation infrastructure, in order to manage traffic volume. Many people commute on a daily basis, so having efficient public transport is crucial in order to improve quality of life.*

The whole paragraph would look like this:

*Living far away from work forces people to commute on a daily basis, which contributes to the second issue, traffic congestion. Traffic congestion has become a critical issue in several cities worldwide. In Shanghai, for example, if you want to go from the East to the West, you may end up spending seven hours sitting in your car due to traffic jams. Something governments must improve is transportation infrastructure, in order to manage traffic volume. Many people commute on a daily basis, so having efficient public transport is crucial in order to improve quality of life.*

## Body Paragraph 3

**In this final body paragraph, we discuss the third issue and solution in the same way as we did with the other two body paragraphs...**

*Overpopulation and excessive traffic lead to pollution, which is the third issue to be addressed. As a result of the high population density in cities, air and water pollution issues are more prominent when compared to rural areas. This can lead to numerous health risks and can reduce quality of life. Local governments could encourage residents to be more mindful of the environment through events and information campaigns, for instance.*

*Another possible solution is the implementation of car-free zones. This initiative has already been launched in several major cities worldwide, and it has had a significant impact on air quality.*

## Conclusion

### Summarize general topic:

*__In summary__, population growth in cities around the world is causing several issues.*

### Summarize solutions:

*To address them, we should do everything we can to offer affordable housing in urban areas, improve transportation, and make people aware of the impact that our lifestyle can have on the environment.*

## Special Vocabulary

- *Moving= relocating*

- *A better life= better quality of life*

- *housing shortages= a lack of suitable housing*

- *potential solutions= possible fixes*

- *dense concentration of people= overpopulation*

- *on a daily basis= daily = every day*

- *excessive traffic= too much traffic = traffic congestion*

- *the third issue to be addressed= To address an issue*

- *car-free zones = no-car zones*

## Notes Section

# Revision Exercise 1

Fill the gaps with an appropriate word or phrase from the box:

| However, | shortages | traffic congestion. | As a result of the high population density |
|---|---|---|---|
| excessive | can lead to numerous | As a first step, | In summary, |
| is the implementation of | lifestyle | To address them, | you may end up |
| Firstly, | commute | issues | in order to manage traffic volume |
| solutions | A growing number of | several | Overpopulation |

# Master IELTS Writing Band 9 Essays

## Model Essay 1

**The number of people moving from rural to urban areas in search of a better life is increasing, but city life comes with its own set of issues.**

**What exactly are these issues, and how can they be solved?**

..................... *people are relocating from rural to urban areas in search of a better quality of life. .................. problems such as housing ..........., traffic congestion, and pollution can have a serious impact on that quality of life. This essay will examine these ............. and propose potential .....................*

*................. the dense concentration of people in cities has resulted in a shortage of affordable housing. In ............ large cities, for example, a large number of people end up living in the suburbs since the shortage of space means renting in the city is too expensive. Living far away from work forces people to ................ on a daily basis, which contributes to the second issue, ..................... Traffic congestion has become a critical issue in several cities worldwide. In Shanghai, for example, if you want to go from the East to the West, .......................... spending seven hours sitting in your car due to traffic jams. ................... and ................. traffic lead to pollution,*

137

*which is the third issue to be addressed. .......................... in cities, air and water pollution issues are more prominent when compared to rural areas. This ................. health risks and can reduce quality of life.*

*................. governments should provide more affordable housing in city centers. UK cities like Manchester and London, for example, have government housing near the city centers to assist low-income families. Another thing that the government must improve is transportation infrastructure, ............................. Many people commute on a daily basis, so having efficient public transport is crucial in order to improve quality of life. Finally, local governments could encourage residents to be more mindful of the environment through events and information campaigns, for instance. Another possible solution ......................... car-free zones. This initiative has already been launched in several major cities worldwide, and it has had a significant impact on air quality.*

*..................... population growth in cities around the world is causing several issues. ............... we should do everything we can to offer affordable housing in urban areas, improve transportation, and make people aware of the impact that our ............... can have on the environment.*

# Revision Exercise 2

Wait for at least 24 hours after you have completed Exercise 1, and then complete the following exercise.

Fill the gaps with an appropriate word or phrase from the box:

| dense | quality of life | since | , for example, |
|---|---|---|---|
| on | on | which | worldwide |
| to | is | so | risks |
| on a | encourage | significant | on |
| affordable | aware of | free | |

Marc Roche

## Model Essay 2

**The number of people moving from rural to urban areas in search of a better life is increasing, but city life comes with its own set of issues.**

**What exactly are these issues, and how can they be solved?**

*A growing number of people are relocating from rural to urban areas in search of a better ................. However, problems such as housing shortages, traffic congestion, and pollution can have a serious impact ..... that quality of life. This essay will examine these issues and propose potential solutions.*

*Firstly, the ................... concentration of people in cities has resulted in a shortage of affordable housing. In several large cities, for example, a large number of people end up living in the suburbs ....... the shortage of space means renting in the city is too expensive. As a first step, governments should provide more affordable housing in city centers. UK cities like Manchester and London............ have government housing near the city centers to assist low-income families.*

*Living far away from work forces people to commute ...... a daily basis, ....... contributes to the second issue, traffic congestion. Traffic congestion has become a critical issue in several cities*

140

# Master IELTS Writing Band 9 Essays

……….. *In Shanghai, for example, if you want to go from the East to the West, you may end up spending seven hours sitting in your car due …… traffic jams. Something governments must improve …… transportation infrastructure, in order to manage traffic volume. Many people commute ………. daily basis, …. having efficient public transport is crucial in order to improve quality of life.*

*Overpopulation and excessive traffic lead to pollution, which is the third issue to be addressed. As a result of the high population density in cities, air and water pollution issues are more prominent when compared to rural areas. This can lead to numerous health ……….. and can reduce quality of life. Local governments could ………. residents to be more mindful of the environment through events and information campaigns, for instance. Another possible solution is the implementation of car-…… zones. This initiative has already been launched in several major cities worldwide, and it has had a ………….. impact …… air quality.*

*In summary, population growth in cities around the world is causing several issues. To address them, we should do everything we can to offer …………. housing in urban areas, improve transportation, and make people ………… the impact that our lifestyle can have on the environment.*

141

## Asnwers: Full Sample Essays

### <u>Sample Structure 1</u>

**The number of people moving from rural to urban areas in search of a better life is increasing, but city life comes with its own set of issues.**

**What exactly are these issues, and how can they be solved?**

*A growing number of people are relocating from rural to urban areas in search of a better quality of life. However, problems such as housing shortages, traffic congestion, and pollution can have a serious impact on that quality of life. This essay will examine these issues and propose potential solutions.*

*Firstly, the dense concentration of people in cities has resulted in a shortage of affordable housing. In several large cities, for example, a large number of people end up living in the suburbs since the shortage of space means renting in the city is too expensive. Living far away from work forces people to commute on a daily basis, which contributes to the second issue, traffic congestion. Traffic congestion has become a critical issue in several cities worldwide. In Shanghai, for example, if you want to go from the East to the West, you may end up spending seven hours sitting in your car due to traffic jams. Overpopulation and excessive traffic lead to pollution, which is the third issue to be addressed. As a result of the high population density in cities, air and water pollution issues are more prominent when compared to rural areas. This can lead to numerous health risks and can reduce quality of life.*

*As a first step, governments should provide more affordable housing in city centers. UK cities like Manchester and London, for example, have government housing near the city centers to assist low-income families. Another thing that the government must improve is transportation infrastructure, in order to manage traffic volume. Many people commute on a daily basis, so having efficient public transport is crucial in order to improve quality of life. Finally, local governments could encourage residents to be more mindful of the environment through events and information campaigns, for instance. Another possible solution is the implementation of car-free zones. This initiative has already been launched in several major cities worldwide, and it has had a significant impact on air quality.*

*In summary, population growth in cities around the world is causing several issues. To address them, we should do everything we can to offer affordable housing in urban areas, improve transportation, and make people aware of the impact that our lifestyle can have on the environment.*

## Sample Structure 2

**The number of people moving from rural to urban areas in search of a better life is increasing, but city life comes with its own set of issues.**

**What exactly are these issues, and how can they be solved?**

*A growing number of people are relocating from rural to urban areas in search of a better quality of life. However, problems such as housing shortages, traffic congestion, and pollution can have a serious impact on that quality of life. This essay will examine these issues and propose potential solutions.*

*Firstly, the dense concentration of people in cities has resulted in a shortage of affordable housing. In several large cities, for example, a large number of people end up living in the suburbs since the shortage of space means renting in the city is too expensive. As a first step, governments should provide more affordable housing in city centers. UK cities like Manchester and London, for example, have government housing near the city centers to assist low-income families.*

*Living far away from work forces people to commute on a daily basis, which contributes to the second issue, traffic congestion. Traffic congestion has become a critical issue in several cities worldwide. In Shanghai, for example, if you want to go from the East to the West, you may end up spending seven hours sitting in your car due to traffic jams. Something governments must improve is transportation infrastructure, in order to manage traffic volume. Many people commute on a daily basis, so having efficient public transport is crucial in order to improve quality of life.*

*Overpopulation and excessive traffic lead to pollution, which is the third issue to be addressed. As a result of the high population density in cities, air and water pollution issues are more prominent when compared to rural areas. This can lead to numerous health risks and can reduce quality of life. Local governments could encourage residents to be more mindful of the environment through events and information campaigns, for instance. Another possible solution is the implementation of car-free zones. This initiative has already been launched in several major cities worldwide, and it has had a significant impact on air quality.*

*In summary, population growth in cities around the world is causing several issues. To address them, we should do everything we can to offer affordable housing in urban areas, improve transportation, and make people aware of the impact that our lifestyle can have on the environment.*

# Discussion Essay

## Typical Question Phrases

*"Discuss both opinions and give your view."*

## Full Task Example:

*Some people believe that single-sex schools are more beneficial to students because they achieve better academic results. Others, however, argue that mixed schools are better since students can develop better social skills.*

*Discuss both views and give your own opinion.*

**Tactics:**

- Write about both sides

- Give a clear opinion

- It doesn't matter what your opinion is, as long as it's clear.

- It's important that your opinion is consistent with what you have written. This means that **it must be a logical opinion based on what you have evaluated.**

# General Structure

### Introduction

- Paraphrase Question and/or state both viewpoints.

- Let the examiner know what you will write about in the main body paragraphs (also called an 'outline sentence')

- Give your main opinion in one sentence (also called 'thesis statement').

### Body Paragraph 1

1. State first viewpoint

2. Discuss the first viewpoint with example if applicable

### Body Paragraph 2

1. State second viewpoint

2. Discuss the second viewpoint with an example if applicable.

### Body Paragraph 3

1. The reason why you agree or disagree with one viewpoint

2. Example or argument to support your view

3. The reason why you agree or disagree with the other viewpoint.

4. Example or argument to support your opinion.

### Conclusion

Sentence 1- Give a summary of your essay here

Sentence 2- Say which side of the argument you agree with

## Common Mistakes

These are the most common mistakes that students make in IELTS discussion essays.

- **Not stating your opinion clearly enough so that the examiner understands it.**

- **Not writing about both sides of the argument.**

- **Not giving both sides of the argument equal attention.**

# How To Plan IELTS Discussion Essays

### Step 1: Analyse the question

This is a crucial part of the planning process and will help you answer the question properly and get an advanced grade (Bands 7-9).

The secret is to identify three different types of words:

- **General Topic words**

- **Subtopic words**

- **Instruction words**

Let's analyse the following exam question:

*Some people believe that single-sex schools are more beneficial to students because they achieve better academic results. Others, however, argue that mixed schools are better since students can develop better social skills.*

*Discuss both views and give your own opinion.*

**Topic words: describe the general subject of the question.**

*Some people believe that **single-sex schools** are more beneficial to students*

151

# Marc Roche

*because they achieve better academic results. Others, however, argue that* **mixed schools** *are better since students can develop better social skills.*

So, the question is about 'single-sex and mixed schools.'

Many IELTS candidates write about the topic in general when they get this type of essay in the test. This is wrong.

We have to identify <u>what sub-topic</u> related to 'single-sex and mixed schools' the examiner wants us to write about.

**Subtopic words** in the question tell us the exact topic we need to focus on.

*Some people believe that* **single-sex schools are more beneficial to students because they achieve better academic results.** *Others, however, argue that* **mixed schools are better since students can develop better social skills.**

By identifying these words, we see that we're being asked about two opposite opinions. These two opinions are that single-sex schools are more beneficial to students because they achieve better academic results and that mixed schools are better since students often develop better social skills. Your essay needs to focus **ONLY** on these subtopics.

**Instruction words:** As we've already looked at in previous essays, instruction words are the actual question words that we will be paraphrasing. In the case of the example above, the instruction words are:

*Discuss both views and give your own opinion.*

### Step 2: Decide on your opinion

Take the easiest opinion to write about!

The examiner doesn't care if you actually agree with the views you express in your essay or not. They care about the level of English you show. You will not be evaluated on any opinion you express, as long as it's expressed logically and in a well-structured manner.

So, choose your opinion and make sure it's clear throughout your essay.

In this example, we are going to say that mixed schools are better.

# Introduction

Essay Question:

*Some people believe that single-sex schools are more beneficial to students because they achieve better academic results. Others, however, argue that mixed schools are better since students can develop better social skills.*

153

## Marc Roche

*Discuss both views and give your own opinion.*

Plan:

1. Paraphrase Question and/or state both viewpoints.

2. Let the examiner know what you will write about in the main body paragraphs (also called an 'outline sentence').

3. Your main opinion in one sentence (also called 'thesis statement')

### 1st - Paraphrase the Issue

**_There is an ongoing debate as to whether the advantages of_** *single-sex schools* **_outweigh the advantages of_** *mixed schools.*

### 2nd Tell the examiner what you will discuss in the main body paragraphs

**_While proponents of_** *single-sex schools argue that children achieve better academic results when learning with their own gender,* **_many people believe that_** *mixed schools help* **_sharpen_** *children's social skills* **to a higher degree.**

### 3rd – Give Opinion

*Although both sides make very valid points, I would argue that mixed schools are better for most children, since they offer.*

Therefore, the introduction paragraph will look like this:

*There is an ongoing debate as to whether the advantages of single-sex schools outweigh the advantages of mixed schools. While proponents of single-sex schools argue that children achieve better academic results when learning with their own gender, many people believe that mixed schools help sharpen children's social skills to a higher degree. Although both sides make very valid points, I would argue that mixed schools are better for most children.*

## Body Paragraph 1

Plan:

1. State first viewpoint

2. Discuss the first viewpoint with example if applicable

**This 1st sentence connects back to the question and signals what we are going to talk about.**

# Marc Roche

*On the one hand, it could be argued that* mixed schools offer a more natural environment where students can learn side-by-side with the opposite sex.

**Discuss the first viewpoint with example if applicable**

*This way,* children can learn to interact and collaborate with their peers **regardless of** gender. This often creates healthier long-term relations with people of the opposite gender. **Furthermore, it is often claimed that** mixed schools can provide students with improved **conflict management skills.** They are more likely to be exposed to a **broader range** of opinions **regarding** social, political, and gender issues. **They will, in theory,** learn to **better manage** disagreements with both genders.

Therefore, the first body paragraph will look like this....

*On the one hand, it could be argued that mixed schools offer a more natural environment where students can learn side-by-side with the opposite sex. This way, children can learn to interact and collaborate with their peers regardless of gender. This often creates healthier long-term relations with people of the opposite gender. Furthermore, it is often claimed that mixed schools can provide students with improved conflict management skills. They are more likely to be exposed to a broader range of opinions regarding social, political, and gender issues. They will, in theory, learn to better manage disagreements with both genders.*

## Body Paragraph 2

Plan:

1. State second viewpoint

2. Discuss the second viewpoint with an example if applicable.

**State second viewpoint**

*__On the other hand, in some cases,__ single-sex schools have fewer distractions __and will therefore__ produce better academic results.*

**Discuss the second viewpoint with an example if applicable.**

*This has actually been proven in some schools, and it is definitely something worth considering. Students who achieve higher grades will often go on to become more successful in life, leading to **greater prosperity** in many cases, **greater career satisfaction.***

## Body Paragraph 3

**Give your opinion here…**

Plan:

1. The reason why you agree or disagree with the first or second viewpoint

2. Example or argument to support your view

3. The reason why you agree or disagree with the first or second viewpoint.

4. Example or argument to support your view

**Outline the reason why you disagree with the argument in favor of single-sex schools**

***However, in my opinion,** students can be equally distracted by members of the opposite sex, **regardless of whether** they are physically present in the classroom **or not**.*

**Example or argument to support your view**

*Students cannot avoid interacting with members of the other sex in their everyday lives. **Therefore, it seems counterintuitive to** segregate them in school.*

# Master IELTS Writing Band 9 Essays

**Outline reason why you agree with the argument in favour of mixed schools**

> *An  added  benefit  of  mixed  schools  is  that  they  enable  students  to  interact and  co-exist  with  the  other gender in a real-life environment...*

**Example or argument to support your view**

> *... where they can learn the **personal boundaries** that must be respected, and they can develop a **more profound sense** of connection and empathy.*

## Conclusion

Plan:

Sentence 1- Summary of the issue

Sentence 2- State which side of the discussion you agree with and why.

**Summary**

> *In conclusion, I firmly believe that developing superior social skills is far more critical to overall long-term success and happiness than*

159

*academic achievement, especially during childhood.. It is also unrealistic to assume that we can eliminate natural distractions from the classroom.*

**State which side of the discussion you agree with:**

*<u>As a result,</u> I agree with the proponents of mixed schools.*

So, the whole conclusion paragraph can look like this:

*<u>In conclusion, I firmly believe</u> that developing superior social skills is **far more critical to overall long-term** success and happiness than academic achievement, especially during childhood.. It is also unrealistic to assume that we can eliminate natural distractions from the classroom. <u>As a result,</u> I agree with the proponents of mixed schools.*

## Special Vocabulary

*Sharpen* children's social skills **to a higher degree**

children can learn to interact and collaborate with their peers **regardless of** gender.

*Improved* **conflict management skills.**

*A* **broader range** of opinions **regarding** social, political, and gender issues.

*They will, in theory,...*

*greater prosperity*

*greater career satisfaction*

*Give your opinion...*

**regardless of whether** they are physically present in the classroom **or not.**

*it seems counterintuitive to segregate* them in school

they **enable** students **to** interact and **co-exist**

*personal boundaries*

*a* **more profound sense** of connection and empathy

## Notes Section

# Master IELTS Writing Band 9 Essays

## Revision Exercise

Fill the gaps with an appropriate word or phrase from the box:

| | | | |
|---|---|---|---|
| *many people believe that* | *sharpen* | *to a higher degree* | *On the one hand, it could be argued that* |
| *regardless of* | *Furthermore, it is often claimed that* | *broader range* | *regarding* |
| *They will, in theory,* | *to better manage* | *However, in my opinion,* | *or not* |
| *regardless of whether* | *and will therefore* | *outweigh the advantages of* | *Therefore, it seems counterintuitive* |
| *There is an ongoing debate as to whether the advantages of* | *While proponents of* | *On the other hand, in some cases,* | *An added benefit of* |
| ***far more critical to overall long-term*** | | | |

163

## Model Essay

Some people believe that single-sex schools are more beneficial to students because they achieve better academic results. Others, however, argue that mixed schools are better since students can develop better social skills.

Discuss both views and give your own opinion.

.................................................... *single-sex schools* .................................... *mixed schools.* .................................... *single-sex schools argue that children achieve better academic results when learning with their own gender,* .................................... *mixed schools help* .................. *children's social skills* .......................... *Although both sides make very valid points, I would argue that mixed schools are better for most children.*

.................................................... *mixed schools offer a more natural environment where students can learn side-by-side with the opposite sex. This way, children can learn to interact and collaborate with their peers* .......................... *gender. This often creates healthier long-term relations with people of the opposite gender. ..................................................... mixed schools can provide students with improved conflict management skills. They are more likely to be exposed to a ............................. of opinions .................... social, political, and gender issues. ............................... learn .................................. .............. disagreements with both genders.*

*...................................................... single-sex schools have fewer distractions ........................................ produce better academic results. This has actually been proven in some schools, and it is definitely something worth considering. Students who achieve higher grades will often go on to become more successful in life, leading to greater prosperity in many cases, greater career satisfaction.*

*....................................... students can be equally distracted by members of the opposite sex, ................................ they are physically present in the classroom ................ Students cannot avoid interacting with members of the other sex in their everyday lives. .................................................. to segregate them in school. ............................ mixed schools is that they enable students to interact and co-exist with the other gender in a real-life environment where they can learn the personal boundaries that*

*must be respected, and they can develop a more profound sense of connection and empathy.*

*In conclusion, I firmly believe that developing superior social skills is ............................... success and happiness than academic achievement, especially during childhood. It is also unrealistic to assume that we can eliminate natural distractions from the classroom. As a result, I agree with the proponents of mixed schools.*

# Answers: Full Sample Essay

Some people believe that single-sex schools are more beneficial to students because they achieve better academic results. Others, however, argue that mixed schools are better since students can develop better social skills.

**Discuss both views and give your own opinion.**

*There is an ongoing debate as to whether the advantages of single-sex schools outweigh the advantages of mixed schools. While proponents of single-sex schools argue that children achieve better academic results when learning with their own gender, many people believe that mixed schools help sharpen children's social skills to a higher degree. Although both sides make very valid points, I would argue that mixed schools are better for most children.*

*On the one hand, it could be argued that mixed schools offer a more natural environment where students can learn side-by-side with the opposite sex. This way, children can learn to interact and collaborate with their peers regardless of gender. This often creates healthier long-term relations with people of the opposite gender. Furthermore, it is often claimed that mixed schools can provide students with improved conflict management skills. They are more likely to be exposed to a broader range of opinions regarding social, political, and gender issues. They will, in theory, learn to better manage disagreements with both genders.*

*On the other hand, in some cases, single-sex schools have fewer distractions and will therefore produce better academic results. This has actually been proven in some schools, and it is definitely something worth considering. Students who achieve higher grades will often go on to become more successful in life, leading to greater prosperity in many cases, greater career satisfaction.*

*However, in my opinion, students can be equally distracted by members of the opposite sex, regardless of whether they are physically present in the classroom or not. Students cannot avoid interacting with members of the other sex in their everyday lives. Therefore, it seems counterintuitive to segregate them in school. An added benefit of mixed schools is that they enable students to interact and co-exist with the other gender in a real-life environment where they can learn the personal boundaries that must be respected, and they can develop a more profound sense of connection and empathy.*

*In conclusion, I firmly believe that developing superior social skills is far more critical to overall long-term success and happiness than academic achievement, especially during childhood. It is also unrealistic to assume that we can eliminate natural distractions from the classroom. As a result, I agree with the proponents of mixed schools.*

# Two-Part Essay Question

# Full Question Example:

This type of essay asks you to answer TWO questions.

*Nowadays, people eat food from different parts of the world, not only local food. What do you think is driving this habit? Is this a good or bad development? Give reasons for your answer and include any relevant examples from your own knowledge or experience.*

# General Structure

You can plan your essay as follows:

## Introduction:

1- Paraphrase the first part of the question to summarise the general topic.

2- Write a sentence to tell the examiner what you will write about.

## Body Paragraph 1

1- Answer 1st question

2- Give a realistic example(s) with a world view

## Body Paragraph 2

1- Answer 2nd question

2- Give a realistic example(s) with a world view

## Conclusion

1- Sentence 1- Summary of reasons for your opinion

2- Sentence 2- State opinion clearly again.

Easy-peasy!

# Common Mistakes

- Not completely answering both questions.

- Not identifying both answers in the essay introduction.

# Brainstorming Ideas

Let's look at an example of how you could plan this essay.

**Nowadays, an increasing number of young people are using the Internet to socialize.**

## What do you think is driving this habit?

- Pandemic

- Teleworking, online banking, etc. Our lives are more and more online, so why not socializing?

- Lack of time

- Less emphasis on social skills and more emphasis on technology at school?

- The emergence of social media has made it more and more acceptable to socialize online

## Do you believe this is positive or negative?

- No, it needs to be controlled.

- Cyberbullying

# You Only Need One or Two Ideas!

- You only need one or two ideas!

- There is a lot of information to write about this topic, so we need to make sure that we keep our writing under control here!

- We have TWO questions to answer, not one!

- So we have to use fewer ideas.

- Choose one main idea for each question.

- Choose ideas that are easy to think of examples for.

## Introduction

Plan:

- Paraphrase the issue

- Outline sentence – give your answer to both questions (a sentence to tell the examiner what you will write about)

### Question:

*Nowadays, an increasing number of young people are using the Internet to socialize.*

*What do you think is driving this habit? Do you believe this is positive or negative? Give reasons for your answer and include any relevant examples from your own knowledge or experience.*

### 1st - Paraphrase the Issue

*At present, there are* **increasingly** *more people* **under the age of thirty** *who are* **turning to** *the internet to socialize.*

### 2nd – Write a sentence to tell the examiner what you will write about.

*This essay will discuss two of the main driving forces behind this behavior and the main reasons why I believe it is mostly a negative trend.*

So, the full introduction looks like this on paper:

*At present, there are increasingly more people under the age of thirty who are turning to the internet to socialize. This essay will discuss two of the main driving forces behind this behavior and the main reasons why I believe it is mostly a negative trend.*

# Master IELTS Writing Band 9 Essays

# Body Paragraph 1

Plan:

1-  Answer 1st question

2-  Give a realistic example(s) with a world view

## 1st Answer 1st question

***Firstly, it is reasonable to assume that*** *one of the main driving forces behind the rise in online socializing is the **advent** of social media in the last two decades. Digital natives have grown up being able to communicate with people from all over the world through direct messages, photographs, voice chat, and video. This has arguably shaped the way they interact and has shifted more of their social connections online. In addition to the influence of social media, young people have had to deal with unprecedented situations, such as the 2008 financial crisis or the more recent COVID 19 pandemic.*

## 2nd Give a realistic example(s) with a world view

*While the 2008 financial crisis led to many young people being unable to find work and spending extended periods of time at home, the COVID 19 pandemic left much of the world's population effectively house-bound for weeks, and in some cases, months **on end**. This meant that people had to adapt, as they had to do all of their socializing online.*

So, the full-body paragraph looks like this on paper:

175

*Firstly, it is reasonable to assume that one of the main driving forces behind the rise in online socializing is the advent of social media in the last two decades. Digital natives have grown up being able to communicate with people from all over the world through direct messages, photographs, voice chat, and video. This has arguably shaped the way they interact and has shifted more of their social connections online. In addition to the influence of social media, young people have had to deal with unprecedented situations, such as the 2008 financial crisis or the more recent COVID 19 pandemic. While the 2008 financial crisis led to many young people being unable to find work and spending extended periods of time at home, the COVID 19 pandemic left much of the world's population effectively house-bound for weeks, and in some cases, months on end. This meant that people had to adapt, as they had to do all of their socializing online.*

*Master IELTS Writing Band 9 Essays*

# Body Paragraph 2

Plan:

1- Answer 2nd question

2- Give a realistic example(s) with a world view

## 1st Answer 2nd question

### Reason 1 for opinion

Answer to question: *Although there are many benefits to socializing online, and it has proven to be highly advantageous in extreme situations such as the pandemic, it is mostly a negative trend when it is overused, in my opinion.*

### Reason 2 for opinion

*Another issue is young people who socialize online have fewer opportunities to practice their interpersonal skills. ...............................*

*This can lead to anti-social behaviors and depression, as they lose real social connections and feel increasingly isolated.*

## 2nd Give a realistic example(s) with a world view

### A real-world example for Reason 1

*For starters, cyberbullying is a major threat to the well-being of both children and adolescents. Cyberbullying occurs on a regular basis on platforms such as Instagram and Facebook, and the rate of suicide among* *teenagers* **is arguably on the rise as a result of this phenomenon.**

### A real-world example for Reason 2

*Users are increasingly texting one another on Facebook and Whatsapp rather than socializing in person.*

So, the second full body paragraph looks like this on paper:

*Although there are many benefits to socializing online, and it has proven to be highly advantageous in extreme situations such as the pandemic, it is mostly a negative trend when it is overused, in my opinion. For starters, cyberbullying is a major threat to the well-being of both children and adolescents. Cyberbullying occurs on a regular basis on platforms such as Instagram and Facebook, and the rate of suicide among teenagers is arguably on the rise as a result of this phenomenon. Another issue is young people who socialize online have fewer opportunities to practice their interpersonal skills. Users are increasingly texting one another on Facebook and Whatsapp rather than socializing in person. This can lead to anti-social behaviors and depression, as they lose real social connections and feel increasingly isolated.*

# Conclusion

Plan:

1- Sentence 1- Summary of reasons for your opinion

2- Sentence 2- State opinion clearly again.

### Summary of reasons for your opinion

*In conclusion, socializing online, if overused, can affect young people's mental health as well as their quality of life.*

### State opinion clearly again to finish

*This is why I believe that online socializing is mostly* **detrimental.**

So, the conclusion paragraph looks like this on paper:

*In conclusion, socializing online, if overused, can affect young people's mental health as well as their quality of life. This is why I believe that online socializing is mostly detrimental.*

## Special Vocabulary

*there are increasingly more people*

*under the age of thirty*

*turning to the internet to socialize.*

*the main driving forces*

*a negative trend*

*it is reasonable to assume that*

*the advent of social media in the last two decades*

*Digital natives*

*has shifted more of their social connections online*

*In addition to the influence of social media,*

*unprecedented situations*

*extended periods of time*

*effectively house-bound*

*for weeks, and in some cases, months on end*

*wellbeing*

*Cyberbullying occurs on a regular basis*

*is arguably on the rise as a result of this phenomenon*

*mostly detrimental*

# Master IELTS Writing Band 9 Essays

## Notes Section

## Revision Exercise

Fill the gaps with an appropriate word or phrase from the box:

| At present, | | under the age of thirty | detrimental. |
|---|---|---|---|
| unable | increasingly | to the influence of social media, | arguably on the rise as a result of this phenomenon |
| turning | effectively house-bound | on end | increasingly |
| arguably shaped | overused | Another issue is | For starters, |
| led to | it is reasonable to assume that | occurs on a regular basis | advent |

### Master IELTS Writing Band 9 Essays

## Model Essay

Nowadays, an increasing number of young people are using the Internet to socialize.

What do you think is driving this habit? Do you believe this is positive or negative? Give reasons for your answer and include any relevant examples from your own knowledge or experience.

*.............. there are ................... more people ...................... who are .............. to the internet to socialize. This essay will discuss two of the main driving forces behind this behavior and the main reasons why I believe it is mostly a negative trend.*

*Firstly, .................................... one of the main driving forces behind the rise in online socializing is the ................... of social media in the last two decades. Digital natives have grown up being able to communicate with people from all over the world through direct messages, photographs, voice chat, and video. This has .................... the way they interact and has shifted more of their social connections online. In addition ......................... young people have had to deal with unprecedented situations, such as the 2008 financial crisis or the more*

183

recent COVID 19 pandemic. While the 2008 financial crisis ………….. many young people being …………… to find work and spending extended periods of time at home, the COVID 19 pandemic left much of the world's population ……………………….. for weeks, and in some cases, months ………………….. This meant that people had to adapt, as they had to do all of their socializing online.

Although there are many benefits to socializing online, and it has proven to be highly advantageous in extreme situations such as the pandemic, it is mostly a negative trend when it is ………….., in my opinion. ………………….. cyberbullying is a major threat to the well-being of both children and adolescents. Cyberbullying ……………………………….. on platforms such as Instagram and Facebook, and the rate of suicide among teenagers is ………………………………………………………………….. ……………………………………. young people who socialize online have fewer opportunities to practice their interpersonal skills. Users are increasingly texting one another on Facebook and Whatsapp rather than socializing in person. This can lead to anti-social behaviors and depression, as they lose real social connections and feel ……………….. isolated.

# Master IELTS Writing Band 9 Essays

*In conclusion, socializing online, if overused, can affect young people's mental health as well as their quality of life. This is why I believe that online socializing is mostly ..........................*

# Answers: Full Sample Essay

Nowadays, an increasing number of young people are using the Internet to socialize.

What do you think is driving this habit? Do you believe this is positive or negative? Give reasons for your answer and include any relevant examples from your own knowledge or experience.

At present, there are increasingly more people under the age of thirty who are turning to the internet to socialize. This essay will discuss two of the main driving forces behind this behavior and the main reasons why I believe it is mostly a negative trend.

Firstly, it is reasonable to assume that one of the main driving forces behind the rise in online socializing is the advent of social media in the last two decades. Digital natives have grown up being able to communicate with people from all over the world through direct messages, photographs, voice chat, and video. This has arguably shaped the way they interact and has shifted more of their social connections online. In addition to the influence of social media, young people have had to deal with unprecedented situations, such as the 2008 financial crisis or the more recent COVID 19 pandemic. While the 2008 financial crisis led to many young people being unable

*Master IELTS Writing Band 9 Essays*

*to find work and spending extended periods of time at home, the COVID 19 pandemic left much of the world's population effectively house-bound for weeks, and in some cases, months on end. This meant that people had to adapt, as they had to do all of their socializing online.*

*Although there are many benefits to socializing online, and it has proven to be highly advantageous in extreme situations such as the pandemic, it is mostly a negative trend when it is overused, in my opinion. For starters, cyberbullying is a major threat to the well-being of both children and adolescents. Cyberbullying occurs on a regular basis on platforms such as Instagram and Facebook, and the rate of suicide among teenagers is arguably on the rise as a result of this phenomenon. Another issue is young people who socialize online have fewer opportunities to practice their interpersonal skills. Users are increasingly texting one another on Facebook and Whatsapp rather than socializing in person. This can lead to anti-social behaviors and depression, as they lose real social connections and feel increasingly isolated.*

*In conclusion, socializing online, if overused, can affect young people's mental health as well as their quality of life. This is why I believe that online socializing is mostly detrimental.*

# IELTS Writing Task 2 Vocabulary & Phrases (Academic & General Training Tests)

### **USEFUL PHRASES**

- If you consider… you could be convinced by an argument in favour of….

- But you have to think about another aspect of the problem…

- I do not feel this is a direct cause of…

- Of course, it goes without saying that…

- There has been a growing body of opinion that…

- … the situation can be addressed by adopting the methods mentioned above…

- While I admit that… I would argue that…

- One approach would be…

- A second possibility would be to…

- Obviously,…

- However,

- This suggests that…

- In addition,…

- To sum up…

- In fact,…

- I tend to disagree…

- I am unconvinced by…

Master IELTS Writing Band 9 Essays

- Overall,…

- In the final analysis…

- Ultimately,…

- To conclude…

- In conclusion…

- On the other hand,…

- There is no doubt that…

- This could involve…

- Thirdly…

## EXPRESSING VIEWS

- I would argue that…

- I firmly believe that…

- It seems to me that...

- I tend to think that…

- People argue that...

- Some people think that…

- Many people feel that…

- In my experience…

- It is undoubtedly true that...

- It is undoubtedly true that….

189

## **REFUTING AN ARGUMENT**

- I am unconvinced that…

- I do not believe that…

- It I hard to accept that…

- It is unjustifiable to say that…

- There is little evidence to support that…

## **PROVIDING SUPPORT**

- For example,…

- For instance,…

- Indeed,…

- In fact,…

- Of course,…

- It can be generally observed that…

- Statistics demonstrate…

- If this is/were the case…

- Firstly,…

- Naturally,…

- In my experience…

- Let me illustrate…

## Master IELTS Writing Band 9 Essays

### **DEFINING/EXPLAINING**

- I would argue that...

- By this I mean...

- In other words,...

- This is to say...

- To be more precise...

- Here I am referring to ...


### **USE SPARINGLY (=a little)**

- First/second, etc....

- Moreover...

- In addition,...

- Furthermore,...

- Nevertheless/nonetheless...

- On the one/other hand...

- Besides...

- Consequently...

- In contrast...

- In comparison...

191

## USE MODERATELY

- While…

- Meanwhile…

- Although…

- In spite of…/ Despite the fact that…

- Even though…

- As a result,…

- However,…

- Since…

- Similarly,…

- Thus…

- In turn

## OTHER USEFUL PHRASES

- My response to this argument depends on what is meant by…

- There is surely a difference between…. and….

- I intend to illustrate how some of these differences are significant to the argument put forward.

- However, whilst I agree that… I am less convinced that…

- I certainly believe that…

- One of the main arguments in favour of…. is that…

- In other words,…

## Master IELTS Writing Band 9 Essays

- Admittedly, in some ways…

- Surely…

- Arguably...

- Either way…

- In any case…

- The most crucial point is that…

- Another point is that…

- Of crucial importance, in my opinion, is…

- There is, however, another possible way of defining…

- …that I am in favour of, although I also realise that…

- Therefore…

- There is no doubt that…

- However, it is possible to tackle this serious issue in several ways.

- One approach would be...

- …would be particularly beneficial.

- A second possibility would be to…

- …this could involve…

- Many people feel that this is unacceptable because…

- Opponents of… point out that … and argue that…

- On the other hand, it cannot be denied that…

- Supporters of…argue that…

## INTRODUCING A FALSE ARGUMENT

- *It could be argued that…*

- *Some people would argue that…*

- *There is also the idea implicit in the statement that…*

- *It is often suggested that…*

## DEMOLISHING A FALSE ARGUMENT

- *This is partly true, but…*

- *To a certain limited extent, there is some truth in this…*

- *However, the implication that… is an oversimplification.*

- *This argument has certain specific logic, but…*

## PROPOSING A CORRECT ARGUMENT

- *It is clear that…*

- *The real situation…*

- *Obviously…*

- *On the contrary…*

- *It is therefore entirely wrong to suggest that…*

## REMEMBER! AN ESSAY CONTAINS:

### INTRO

- ✓ *About 50 words*
- ✓ *A general statement about the topic*
- ✓ *The purpose of the essay*
- ✓ *Initial views of the writer on the subject*

### BODY

- ✓ *About 170 words*
- ✓ *Develops the key ideas and the topic mentioned in the intro*
- ✓ *consist of 2-3 paragraphs*
- ✓ *related to the opening and closing paragraphs*

### CONCLUSION

- ✓ 30-40 words
- ✓ No new info!
- ✓ sums up the key points covered in the essay

# REMEMBER!

- Read the questions very carefully.

- Underline key points in the question and make sure it is relevant to these.

- Consider your personal view on the topic. Do you disagree/ agree or have an impartial view?

- Take a minute to PLAN what you are going to say in your answer.

- Think of the main idea you will introduce in each paragraph, then think of some supporting points.

- Before you start writing, think about how you will introduce the topic.

- Do not copy the question!!!

- Introduce some arguments that are relevant to your society or personal experience.

- Clearly state your conclusion. Make sure that you address the question.

- Read through your answer when you have finished and check grammar, spelling, and punctuation.

- Check that you have liked your points together well.

- Make sure you have written enough words. No less than 250!!!

# Master IELTS Writing Band 9 Essays

**When you have finished writing your essay, check what you have written by answering these questions:**

- ☑ Is the length of the text appropriate?

- ☑ Does the text answer the question?

- ☑ Are there any errors in the text? If there are, what are they?

- ☑ Is there an excessive repetition of any words or phrases?

- ☑ Is anything missing?

- ☑ Are the paragraphs well linked together? If so, in what way?

- ☑ Does your essay include a range of vocabulary and structures?

# IELTS- WRITING - TASK 2

## Useful Phrases

- I do not feel this is a direct cause of…

- Of course, it goes without saying that…

- There has been a growing body of opinion that...

- … the situation can be addressed by adopting the methods mentioned above…

- While I admit that… I would argue that…

- One approach would be…

- A second possibility would be to…

- Obviously,…

- However,

- This suggests that…

- In addition,…

- To sum up…

- In fact...

- I tend to disagree…

- I am unconvinced by…

# Master IELTS Writing Band 9 Essays

- Overall,…

- In the final analysis…

- Ultimately,…

- To conclude…

- In conclusion…

- On the other hand,…

- There is no doubt that…

- This could involve…

- Thirdly…

## Expressing Views

- I would argue that…

- I firmly believe that…

- It seems to me that...

- I tend to think that…

- People argue that...

- Some people think that…

- Many people feel that…

- In my experience…

- It is undoubtedly true that...

- It is certainly true that....

## Refuting an Argument

- I am unconvinced that...

- I do not believe that...

- It I hard to accept that...

- It is unjustifiable to say that...

- There is little evidence to support that...

## Providing Support

- For example,...

- For instance,...

- Indeed,...

- In fact,...

- Of course,...

- It can be generally observed that...

- Statistics demonstrate...

_Master IELTS Writing Band 9 Essays_

- If this is/were the case…

- Firstly,…

- Naturally,…

- In my experience…

- Let me illustrate…

## Defining and Explaining

- I would argue that…

- By this I mean…

- In other words...

- This is to say…

- To be more precise...

- Here I am referring to …

## Use These Carefully

- First/second, etc.…

- Moreover...

- In addition,…

- Furthermore,…

- Nevertheless/nonetheless…

- On the one/other hand…

- Besides…

- Consequently…

- In contrast…

- In comparison…

## Use Moderately

- While…

- Meanwhile…

- Although…

- In spite of…/ Despite the fact that…

- Even though…

- As a result,…

- However,…

- Since…

- Similarly,…

- Thus…

- In turn

# Master IELTS Writing Band 9 Essays

## Other Useful Phrases

- My response to this argument depends on what is meant by…

- There is surely a difference between…. and….

- I intend to illustrate how some of these differences are significant to the argument put forward.

- However, whilst I agree that… I am less convinced that…

- I certainly believe that…

- One of the main arguments in favour of…. is that…

- In other words,…

- Admittedly, in some ways…

- Surely…

- Arguably…

- Either way…

- In any case…

- The most important point is that…

- Another point is that…

- Of crucial importance, in my opinion, is…

- There is, however, another possible way of defining…

- …that I am in favour of, although I also realise that…

- Therefore…

- There is no doubt that…

- However, it is possible to tackle this serious issue in a number of ways.

- One approach would be...

- …would be particularly beneficial.

- A second possibility would be to…

- …this could involve…

- Many people feel that this is unacceptable because…

- Opponents of… point out that … and argue that…

- On the other hand, it cannot be denied that…

- Supporters of…argue that…

## Introducing a False Argument

- It could be argued that...

- Some people would argue that...

- There is also the idea implicit in the statement that...

- It is often suggested that...

## Destroying a False Argument

- This is partly true, but...

- To a certain extent, there is some truth in this..., however,...

- However, the implication that... is an oversimplification.

- This argument has certain specific logic, but...

## Suggesting a Correct Argument

- It is clear that...

- The real situation...

- Obviously...

- On the contrary...

- It is therefore quite wrong to suggest that...

# Private IELTS Writing Advanced BAND 9 Course on ©Udemy

REACH YOUR POTENTIAL IN IELTS WRITING

## IMPRESS WITH YOUR WRITING SKILLS

### ©UDEMY IELTS WRITING COURSE DISCOUNT
https://bit.ly/3OF0v0h

Marc Roche

# FREE IELTS Writing Course: Advanced Writing (Foundation Level for IELTS)

**GET SMART ABOUT IELTS WRITING NOW!**

**Claim your FREE Mini-Course Worth $67 Below!**

https://www.macsonbell.com/ielts-toolbox

Printed in Great Britain
by Amazon